THE MYTH
OF THE
MODERN
PRESIDENCY

THE MYTH
OF THE
MODERN
PRESIDENCY

David K. Nichols

THE PENNSYLVANIA STATE UNIVERSITY PRESS
University Park, Pennsylvania

Library of Congress Cataloging-in-Publication Data

Nichols, David K.
    The myth of the modern presidency / David K. Nichols.
        p.   cm.
    Includes bibliographical references and index.
    ISBN 0–271–01316–8 (alk. paper).—ISBN 0–271–01317–6 (pbk.:
alk. paper)
        1. Presidents—United States. 2. Presidents—United States—
History. I. Title.
JK516.N53 1994
324.6′3′0973—dc20   93–36532
                                                                                              CIP

Published by The Pennsylvania State University Press,
Suite C, Barbara Building, University Park, PA 16802–1003

It is the policy of The Pennsylvania State University Press to use acid-free paper
for the first printing of all clothbound books. Publications on uncoated stock
satisfy the minimum requirements of American National Standard for Information Sciences—Permanence of Paper for Printed Library Materials, ANSI Z39.48–
1984.

Contents

Preface

This work is open to a number of criticisms, the most important of which is that I have been selective in my treatment of the operation and development of the American Presidency. To that charge I must plead guilty. But any attempt to be comprehensive in dealing with such a broad theme necessarily would end in failure. What I have tried to do is to suggest a framework for the study of the Presidency, a framework that differs in some important respects from that offered by other contemporary scholars. The value of that framework will ultimately be established by scholars who will determine if it explains more of the particular history and operation of the Presidency than other assumptions underlying study of the Presidency.

Even this limited effort would not have been possible without a great deal of assistance. I am grateful to the H. B. Earhart Foundation and the Lynde and Harry Bradley Foundation for support for the early stages of this project. Sanford G. Thatcher at The Pennsylvania State University Press has carefully guided the manuscript through review and publication. He is a model for what a press director should be. And, as senior manuscript editor, Peggy Hoover has done much to improve the clarity, consistency, and style of the book. I would also like to acknowledge the helpful suggestions of the anonymous reviewers who have helped me to avoid numerous errors and to clarify a number of my arguments.

More than anyone I know, I am dependent on conversations with others to explore and develop my ideas, and I have been fortunate over the years to have found people willing to listen and talk. From my oldest friend, Don Bradley, with whom I have been arguing about the American Presidency since the Kennedy administration, to my close friends from graduate school at Northern Illinois University and the University of Virginia, I would like to say thank you for tolerating my endless theories and arguments about political life.

I have also been fortunate to have had a number of exceptional teachers. Professor David Broyles first showed me that the study of political philosophy might bring together thought and action or the world of ideas with the most pressing human questions. Professor Morton Frisch managed to assemble a remarkable group of students and teachers in the cornfields of DeKalb, Illinois. Professors Frisch, Martin Diamond, Herbert Storing, and a talented junior professor just out of graduate school offered me an exceptional grounding in political theory and American political thought.

In particular, Professor Storing showed me that the most abstract questions of political philosophy could be seen concretely in the study of American political institutions. Through his teaching and scholarship, I learned how to reconcile my long-standing passion for American politics with my newfound respect for political philosophy. I moved to the University of Virginia in the fall of 1977 to complete my doctoral work with him, anticipating writing a doctoral dissertation on the Presidency under his direction. But that was not to be. What is even more disappointing is that we will never have the book on the Presidency that Professor Storing would have written.

But once again I was lucky. Almost immediately I found one of the most engaging and thoughtful people I have ever met—Professor James Ceaser. Ceaser cares about ideas and about politics, and he has a mind that is as lively as his character. Most important for me, he was willing to put up with an obnoxious graduate student who didn't know when to shut up (and still doesn't). Not only did he manage to guide me through a dissertation on party realignments, but he has continued to be the second most thoughtful critic of my work. Professor Ceaser, as well as Professor William Connelly and Professor Stephen Thomas, read my entire manuscript and made numerous helpful comments. But in the end there is only so much one can do with what one has to work with.

No one appreciates this fact more than my wife. As many of you will have guessed, she is my most thoughtful critic—and that talented young professor I met many years ago in DeKalb. And she is much more. Not only is she a constant reminder to me of the truth and beauty to be found in the world of ideas, but also, and more important, she demonstrates in her work and her life that the world of ideas is not meant to be an escape from the world in which we live. Ideas have meaning only to the extent that they help us to live in this world or to deepen our appreciation of the richness of that existence.

I hope that this book will make some small contribution to an appreciation of the complexity and richness of the ideas that animate the American Presidency.

Introduction

The term "modern Presidency" has become an accepted part of the language of scholars and political commentators. Few people question the idea that the expansive powers of the "modern Presidency" emerged in the twentieth century as an alternative to the cramped legal office created by the Constitution and occupied by nineteenth-century Presidents. One only has to survey contemporary American government textbooks to see the widespread acceptance of the doctrine of the "modern Presidency." For example, Burns, Peltason, and Cronin claim that "the nation's founders created a presidency of somewhat limited powers."[1] In *The American Democracy,* Thomas Patterson contends that "each of the President's constitutional powers has been broadened beyond the Framers' intention."[2] Barbara Hinckley and Sheldon Goldman find that "a spiralling of power occurs over time whereby events and actions of individual Presidents lead

1. James MacGregor Burns, J. W. Peltason, and Thomas E. Cronin, *Government by the People,* 14th ed. (Englewood Cliffs, N.J.: Prentice Hall, 1991), 380.
2. Thomas E. Patterson, *The American Democracy* (New York: McGraw-Hill, 1990), 465.

to expectations by the public and others."[3] And Theodore Lowi and Benjamin Ginsberg explain the development of the Presidency this way:

> A tug of war between formal constitutional provisions favoring a chief clerk president and a theory of necessity favoring a chief executive president has persisted for two centuries. . . . But it was not until Franklin Roosevelt that the tug of war seems to have been won for the chief executive presidency, because after FDR . . . every president was strong whether he was committed to the strong presidency or not.[4]

Another popular American government textbook concludes: "The history of presidential power is one of steady but uneven growth."[5]

Some version of this view, implicitly or explicitly stated, is presented in virtually all American government texts and pervades most political scholarship and political commentary; the powerful modern Presidency had to escape the limits of the constitutional office. The concept of the modern Presidency has become a powerful myth, a myth that embodies much of the contemporary understanding of the development and operation of the political system. Like most myths, the myth of the modern Presidency is not without foundation; it reflects some important aspects of our political experience. But like most myths it is ultimately unsatisfactory because it distorts reality.

It is like more traditional myths in one other respect—it has been accepted largely on faith. There has been little scholarly work devoted to defining and outlining the development of the "modern Presidency." While many works use the term, few bother to provide a precise definition or an account of its origins. The most cited work on the subject is not even a book, but an article by Fred Greenstein entitled "Change and Continuity in the Modern Presidency."[6] Greenstein's article provides the most systematic and concise definition of the modern Presidency to be found, and explains the belief that the modern Presidency emerged during the administration of Franklin Roosevelt.

3. Barbara Hinckley and Sheldon Goldman, *American Politics and Government: Structure, Process, Institutions, and Policies* (Chicago: Scott, Foresman / Little, Brown & Co., 1990), 291.

4. Theodore J. Lowi and Benjamin Ginsberg, *American Government: Freedom and Power* (New York: W. W. Norton & Co., 1990), 243–44.

5. Burns et al., *Government by the People*, 381.

6. Fred I. Greenstein, "Change and Continuity in the Modern Presidency," in *The New American Political System*, ed. Anthony King (Washington, D.C.: American Enterprise Institute, 1978), 45–85.

Greenstein admits that there were variations in the exercise of presidential power in Presidencies before that of Franklin Roosevelt, but he says that with FDR "the Presidency began to undergo not a shift but rather a metamorphosis."[7] Greenstein identifies four areas in which this metamorphosis has taken place. First, the President became actively involved in initiating and seeking congressional support for legislation and consistently used the veto as a means to pursue his legislative agenda. Second, "a President that normally exercised few unilateral powers" became one who makes policy "through executive orders and other actions not formally ratified by Congress." Third, the President created an extensive bureaucracy in the executive office to support his legislative agenda and independent policy-making. Fourth, the office of the Presidency was personalized. "Presidents are expected to be symbols of reassurance, possessing extraordinary 'nonpolitical' personal qualities that were traditionally associated with long deceased 'hero Presidents.'"[8]

Greenstein admits that Presidents such as Andrew Jackson, James Polk, Abraham Lincoln, Grover Cleveland, Theodore Roosevelt, and Woodrow Wilson exhibited many of the attributes of the modern activist Presidency, but he claims that they were the exception rather than the rule. "Except under these assertive leaders, Presidential power was generally weak before 1932."[9] The twin crises of the depression and World War II converged with the "long incumbency of perhaps the most giftedly entrepreneurial President in American history" to permanently transform the office.[10] Harry Truman and Dwight Eisenhower helped to institutionalize the modern Presidency, but it was Franklin Roosevelt who made the transformation possible. According to Greenstein, even in the face of the post-Watergate reforms created to restrain the Presidency, the President not Congress remains the focal point of American government.[11]

Greenstein, however, also suggests a certain ambivalence about the power of the modern Presidency. He reminds us that even Richard Neustadt, author of *Presidential Power*, feared the potential weakness of the modern Presidency. Neustadt thought "presidents would fail to be politically effective because of the restraints placed on them by other elements in the political system and because of their own failure to exercise skilled

7. Ibid., 45.

8. Ibid., 45–46.

9. Fred I. Greenstein, Larry Berman, and Alvin S. Felzenberg, *Evolution of the Modern Presidency: A Bibliographical Survey* (Washington, D.C.: American Enterprise Institute, 1977), ii.

10. Greenstein, "Change and Continuity," 47.

11. ·Greenstein et al., *Evolution of the Modern Presidency*, i.

leadership."[12] Neustadt himself said that the real topic of his book was presidential weakness not presidential strength.[13] He wrote *Presidential Power* in order to encourage Presidents to develop their political skills and take charge of the Presidency and the political system, rather than to rest content with being the chief clerk in a limited constitutional system.

Greenstein agrees that modern Presidents are not inevitably powerful Presidents. Their large staffs, unilateral powers, and attempts to influence the legislative process and symbolize national unity will not automatically be successful. In fact, Greenstein concludes that the expectations for the modern Presidency have far exceeded the possible. Because of this, he calls for a redefinition of the modern Presidency in "more workable terms."

> This role definition would make it perfectly clear that the buck—a term that presumably refers to all major policy-making—neither stops nor starts only in the Oval Office. It circulates among many political actors. Depending upon the President's skill, his interest, the nature of the issues being considered, and the state of the national and international political environment, the President can have a major impact on how the buck circulates and with what results. But he neither is, nor can be, nor should be an unmoved mover.[14]

The model for the modern Presidency, according to Greenstein, should be Eisenhower—not Franklin Roosevelt.[15] The "political skills and widespread sense of crisis that enabled [Franklin Roosevelt] to put them to work were sui generis."[16] The FDR model is not replicable. Although it will be helpful for a President to follow Neustadt's advice and sharpen his political skills, no modern President will succeed unless he manages to lower the expectations for the office.

Greenstein's conclusion, however, should give pause to those who uncritically accept the doctrine of the "modern Presidency." On the one hand, we are told that in the modern period "Presidents have had to be leaders whether they chose to be or not."[17] On the other hand, we are told that the success of the modern Presidency may turn on a President's ability to decide when and *when not* to lead. It is not clear whether Franklin

---

12. Greenstein, "Change and Continuity," 68.

13. Richard Neustadt, *Presidential Power and the Modern Presidents* (New York: The Free Press, 1990), ix.

14. Greenstein, "Change and Continuity," 85.

15. Fred I. Greenstein, *The Hidden-Hand Presidency* (New York: Basic Books, 1982).

16. Greenstein, "Change and Continuity," 83–84.

17. Greenstein et al., *Evolution of the Modern Presidency*, iii.

Roosevelt's model of the modern Presidency is inescapable or whether it is merely a matter of choice.

For example, we do find elements of the modern Presidency in Eisenhower's administration. He pursued a legislative agenda, expanding and reorganizing the legislative liaison office in the White House. He defended unilateral presidential discretion, particularly in his fight against the Bricker Amendment. He created a large hierarchical bureaucracy in the White House, and he relied on his image as war hero to add personal luster to his Presidency. Eisenhower even accepted much of the expanded role for the national government in foreign or domestic affairs. He did not dismantle the national government that had grown up in the New Deal, nor did he remove from the national political agenda the host of issues that had been added since the 1930s.

Nonetheless, Eisenhower's Presidency differed markedly from Franklin Roosevelt's in regard to each of the criteria of the modern Presidency. Eisenhower did pursue a domestic agenda, but its limited character, compared with that of FDR, surely suggests a qualitative as well as a quantitative change. Eisenhower did defend unilateral presidential powers, but few people would describe Eisenhower's tenure as a prerogative Presidency. Eisenhower's White House staff was hierarchical, but much discretion was allowed to remain at the lower levels of the administrative hierarchy. Finally, Eisenhower may have been a hero-President, but few describe his Presidency in heroic terms. He conducted a successful but decidedly nonheroic Presidency. It was, after all, the Eisenhower Presidency that prompted Neustadt to write *Presidential Power* in order to instruct future Presidents to behave more like Franklin Roosevelt.

In this light, how can we speak of a lasting transformation of the office by Roosevelt? If Eisenhower redefined the modern Presidency in a positive manner, as Greenstein argues, why did later Presidents not follow his lead? John Kennedy, Lyndon Johnson, and Richard Nixon, each in their own way, rejected the model of the moderate modern Presidency presented by Eisenhower. Gerald Ford and Jimmy Carter appear to follow neither the FDR model nor the Eisenhower model. They are modern Presidents only to the extent that they fail to live up to the expectations created by the "modern Presidency." But if raised expectations are the most lasting or essential element of the "modern Presidency" then the concept might be reduced to the claim that Franklin Roosevelt was a tough act to follow. Even this claim needs qualification. We must remember that it was scholar Richard Neustadt who was uncomfortable with Eisenhower's failure to emulate FDR. The nation liked Ike, and so does Greenstein.

Of course, one could argue that these are mere qualifications of the modern Presidency thesis. Different aspects of the modern Presidency have been emphasized by different Presidents, and we have had more and less successful modern Presidents. The real question is whether something fundamental changed in the character of the office during Franklin Roosevelt's tenure.

To deny that some important changes took place would be impossible in light of obvious evidence to the contrary. The myth of the modern Presidency correctly identifies some important changes. The President's involvement in the legislative process dramatically increased, and the White House staff was not merely increased but transformed from a few personal aides to a substantial presidential bureaucracy. Executive orders, executive rule-making, and executive agreements provided the most obvious examples of a more general increase in the amount of independent presidential decision-making. Finally, use of the electronic media clearly made the President a more personal presence in the lives of most Americans.

But the myth of the modern Presidency is incorrect in assuming that these changes required a transformation of the constitutional office of the Presidency. The increased activity of the President can be attributed to broad changes in the character of government and society, and not to a change in the balance of power between the President and the other branches. The greater presidential activity in initiating and supporting legislation was the result of the fact that more legislative initiatives and more legislation were now considered to be legitimate and even necessary. The increased White House staff was largely a response to the increase in the legislative and administrative activities of an expanded national government. As the activities of the government increased, the opportunities for executive discretion were multiplied. And as more was expected of the national government, the most visible symbol of the national government, the President, became a more pervasive presence in the public life of the nation.

What did not change, however, was the essential constitutional role of the President. Not only in 1932, but also in 1990, in 1890, and in 1790, the President was responsible for new legislative initiatives, for controlling the bureaucracy, for making unilateral executive decisions, and for serving as a symbol of national unity. The modern Presidency did not just burst on the scene in 1932; it arose much earlier in our history. We have already seen that Greenstein offers a long list of premodern quasi-"modern Presidents" including Jackson, Polk, Lincoln, Cleveland, Theodore Roosevelt, and Wilson. George Washington, Thomas Jefferson, and William McKinley could easily be added to the list. The terms of these Presidents would cover 60 of the first 130 years of the American Presidency. These Presidencies could hardly be considered to be exceptions. Were there weak Presidents during this period? Of course there were. Lincoln, Jackson, and

Jefferson were all tough acts to follow, just as Franklin Roosevelt had been. And as Calvin Coolidge so appropriately noted, "a nation cannot always dwell on the mountaintops." There have been peaks and valleys of presidential leadership throughout our history, and there will continue to be.

All the elements of the modern Presidency were exhibited long before Franklin Roosevelt because their source is the Constitution. The truth behind the myth of the modern Presidency is that recent Presidents do more than previous Presidents, but that is traceable to the simple fact that modern American government as a whole does more. It is this broader change in the extent of government action, not a change in the constitutional balance of power among the branches, that provides some legitimacy to the myth of the modern Presidency. Relative to the tasks that government performs, modern Presidents do no more—and no less— than Presidents have done in the past. The failure to make this distinction has created a great deal of confusion in our understanding of contemporary American politics and has led to a number of misguided reforms and proposals for reform.

That confusion is most evident when we look at recent scholarship on the Presidency. Lyndon Johnson's withdrawal from the 1968 presidential race, the forced resignation of Richard Nixon, and the Presidencies of Gerald Ford and Jimmy Carter raised important questions about the doctrine of the modern Presidency. How could these four Presidencies be reconciled with the notion of the powerful modern Presidency? These questions were soon resolved by the doctrine of the "imperilled Presidency."[18] The doctrine of the modern Presidency was not a mistake. The

18. I use the term "imperilled Presidency" because it seems to be an appropriate counterpoint to the "imperial" Presidency literature of the early 1970s. It serves as a useful umbrella for the various scholars and commentators who emphasized the increasing vulnerability of the modern Presidency. George Reedy, *Twilight of the Presidency* (Cleveland: New American Library, 1970) began to focus on the weaknesses of the modern Presidency in response to the problems of the Johnson administration. But it was in the late 1970s and early 1980s that the idea of the "imperilled Presidency" found its greatest support. James Sterling Young's two articles in the *New York Times* provide a concise formulation of the concept ("The Troubled Presidency: I," *New York Times,* December 6, 1978, A25; "The Troubled Presidency: II," *New York Times,* December 7, 1978, A23). See also Thomas E. Cronin, *The State of the Presidency,* 2d ed. (Boston: Little, Brown & Co., 1980); Vincent Davis, ed., *The Post-Imperial Presidency* (New Brunswick, N.J.: Transaction Books, 1980), particularly the article by Thomas E. Cronin entitled "An Imperilled Presidency?" 137–51; Hugh Heclo and Lester M. Salamon, eds., *The Illusion of Presidential Government* (Boulder, Colo.: Westview Press, 1981); Harold M. Barger, *The Impossible Presidency* (Glenview, Ill.: Scott, Foresman, 1984); and L. Gordon Crovitz and Jeremy Rabkin, eds., *The Fettered Presidency* (Washington, D.C.: American Enterprise Institute, 1989). Most recently, Aaron Wildavsky's collection of essays entitled *The Beleaguered Presidency* (New Brunswick, N.J.: Transaction Publishers, 1991) traces the development of the problems of the modern Presidency from Nixon through Bush.

office had been transformed to heroic proportions. The problem was that the expectations of the modern Presidency had grown so great that no President could fulfill them. The success of the modern Presidency had led to the tragedy of the modern Presidency.

Before the ink had dried on the "imperilled Presidency" literature, Ronald Reagan became president, and scholars and commentators were once again thrown into a state of confusion. If the Presidency were imperilled, why was Reagan enjoying apparent success? We soon learned, however, that reports of a healthy presidential office under Reagan had been greatly exaggerated.

In his 1985 book *The Personal President,* Theodore Lowi explained that Reagan's success while real was partial.[19] Reagan mastered one of the most important elements of the modern Presidency—personal popular leadership. But that success came at a cost, the cost of further raising expectations for the government and the Presidency that must ultimately be disappointed. In 1987 Jeffrey Tulis followed with his book *The Rhetorical Presidency,* which further described the transformation of the presidential office from one of legal and constitutional powers to one based on the power of political rhetoric.[20] According to Tulis, modern Presidents do not turn to the Constitution as a source of power, they turn instead to political rhetoric to build short-term political support. This leads to two dangers. Rhetorical success tends to erode the legal and constitutional limits on presidential power, and in the long run rhetorical success may weaken the Presidency by undermining the stable constitutional and legal supports for presidential power.

Although George Bush was often charged with emphasizing symbols over substance in his 1988 presidential campaign, it soon became obvious that his lack of rhetorical skill was a leading cause of the failure of his Presidency. His failure in the "vision" department led to a renewed appreciation of the importance of the President's role as symbolic leader. Bill Clinton enthusiastically embraced the role of symbolic leader, claiming that he could offer a new vision for American politics. And it was this symbolic or rhetorical leadership that helped to ensure his election. But it is not surprising that the major complaint in the early days of the Clinton administration has been about the gulf between rhetoric and results. In addition, Clinton's stated desire to continue his campaign during his term of office has provided fresh ammunition for those concerned with the potential excesses of the rhetorical Presidency.

19. Theodore J. Lowi, *The Personal President: Power Invested, Promise Unfulfilled* (Ithaca, N.Y.: Cornell University Press, 1985).

20. Jeffrey K. Tulis, *The Rhetorical Presidency* (Princeton: Princeton University Press, 1987).

Presidential scholarship, however, should do more than react to the virtues or shortcomings of our most recent President. To reorient presidential scholarship, we need to show the limitations of the concept of the modern Presidency and to recover an appreciation of the constitutional Presidency. But what are the major differences between the doctrine of the modern Presidency and the theory of the constitutional Presidency? One might argue that the elements of the modern Presidency identified by Greenstein provide a good description of the President's constitutional role. It is my contention that legislative leadership, administrative control, the exercise of unilateral authority, and popular symbolic leadership are all crucial elements of the constitutional Presidency. The major defect of the doctrine of the modern Presidency is the failure to recognize that these attributes of the Presidency predate Franklin Roosevelt and in fact find their origins in the Constitution.

But this defect has implications not only for our interpretation of the history of the Presidency but also for our understanding of the contemporary operation of the constitutional Presidency. By failing to recognize the constitutional origins of the major elements of the modern Presidency, the doctrine of the modern Presidency ignores the extent to which the Constitution shapes contemporary political behavior.[21] It fails to understand the extent to which these elements of the modern Presidency are dependent on specific constitutional provisions. It is this failure to recognize the institutional dynamics of the Constitution that often leads to misguided reforms and proposals for reform.

Also, by associating the rise of a powerful Presidency with the rise of a more active national government, the doctrine of the modern Presidency fails to appreciate the connection between a powerful constitutional Presidency and the idea of limited government. Greenstein and the "imperilled Presidency" school are correct in arguing that unrealistic expectations will lead to cynicism and pose a serious threat to the political system. But they

21. The development of the concept of the modern Presidency has closely paralleled that of another development in presidential scholarship: the emphasis on behavioral as opposed to legal explanations of the Presidency. Ultimately the behavioral approach may be traced to the desire of Progressive scholars to "liberate democracy from the bondage of law" (Herbert Croly, *Progressive Democracy* [New York: Macmillan Co., 1915], 256). The Constitution and the laws served only to restrain presidential power and the power of government as a whole. An active government and an active Presidency can be understood only in extralegal terms. Just as the modern Presidency has developed out of the precedents established by the actions of Presidents rather than the expansion of constitutional powers, the behavioral study of the Presidency rests on the study of what Presidents do, rather than on what the Constitution says they should do. It has rescued us from the irrelevance of what Thomas Cronin and others have called the "textbook Presidency" (Cronin, *The State of the Presidency*, 75–118).

are wrong in focusing their concern on the office of the Presidency. The problem of contemporary American politics is not that we expect too much of the President but that we expect too much of the government. As the most visible symbol of the national government, the President is bound to suffer most from disappointed expectations regarding the performance of the government as a whole. But we will not solve this problem by placing limits on the office of the Presidency or on our expectations of the Presidency. The solution will come only through a reexamination of the ends of government.

The myth of the modern Presidency prevents us from seeing the theory of the constitutional Presidency. It severs the connections between effective presidential leadership and the idea of constitutional government. The purpose of this book is to restore an appreciation of that connection. In the first chapter we shall see that the elements of the modern Presidency associated with Franklin Roosevelt's administration are equally prevalent in earlier administrations. The attributes of the modern Presidency can be found in the early twentieth-century Presidencies of Theodore Roosevelt and Woodrow Wilson, in the nineteenth-century Presidencies of Lincoln and Jackson, and even in the eighteenth-century Presidency of George Washington.

A close study of the Constitution in Chapter 2 shows that the potential for the modern Presidency was created in the Constitution itself. We find "modern" Presidents throughout our history because the essential elements of the modern Presidency, including the President's role as a popular leader, are a logical outgrowth of the decisions made at the Constitutional Convention and embodied in the Constitution.[22]

Chapters 3, 4, and 5 analyze the development of three essential aspects of the modern Presidency. By examining the President's role in the budget process, Chapter 3 explores the President's role as legislative and popular leader. It is this role that is most often associated with the "modern" Presidency and viewed as alien to the constitutional Presidency. But we shall see that the President has historically set the political and legislative agenda and that the failure to recognize that point has led to some serious errors in efforts to reform the budgetary process. By better understanding the constitutional origins of the President's role as opinion leader and agenda setter, we will better understand the failure of recent attempts at budget reform.

Chapter 4 looks at the central function of the President: the President's

---

22. Jeffrey K. Tulis suggests a similar line of argument. See his "The Constitutional Presidency in American Political Development," in *The Constitution and the American Presidency*, ed. Martin Fausold and Alan Shank (Albany, N.Y.: SUNY Press, 1991), 133–46.

role as chief executive. We shall see that even supporters of presidential power in the area of administration have often failed to comprehend fully what it means to speak of an independent executive power. Because of this failure, they have been unable to develop a workable notion of administrative responsibility. The growth of the administrative state is seen as a practically necessary but constitutionally suspect development, and the attempt to place constitutional restraints on such a state is seen as hopelessly anachronistic. By elaborating the meaning of an independent executive power, I hope to overcome both difficulties. I explain that the growth of the administrative state is consistent with the constitutional doctrine of the separation of powers, and that the constitutional separation of powers properly understood provides the best source of restraint for such a state.

Through an analysis of the war powers debate, Chapter 5 investigates the tension between the President's discretionary authority in foreign affairs and the desire to place legal and constitutional restraints on the President's actions. We shall find that ironically it is the opponents of presidential authority who are the actual source of the doctrine of extra-constitutional prerogative powers in foreign affairs, and that it is the defenders of a strong constitutional Presidency who seek to balance the concerns of necessity with those of limited government.

Chapter 6 shows that the problem of reconciling the need for governmental power and discretion with the goal of maintaining a limited popular government is at the core of modern political philosophy. Many current misconceptions of executive power can be traced to confusion over the solution to that problem offered by early modern political thinkers. We shall see that the common thread running from Machiavelli and Hobbes through Locke and Montesquieu is an appreciation of the fact that a powerful independent executive is essential to the maintenance of a limited popular government, and moreover that the doctrine of limited government itself may be a source of executive power and independence.

Finally, in Chapter 7 I argue that it is the authors of the American Constitution, not the English or European political philosophers, who provide the most satisfactory reconciliation of executive power and limited popular government. It is the authors of the Constitution who created the modern Presidency. Although that fact has been obscured first by nineteenth-century American Whigs and later by twentieth-century Progressives, a recovery of the constitutional Presidency will provide the best framework for understanding the past and looking to the future of constitutional government. The Constitution is not some abstract moral or legal code; it is a document that has shaped behavior for more than 200 years. It demonstrates the inextricable link between the *is* and the *ought* of politics and political science.

CHAPTER ONE

The History
of the Modern Presidency

Although the term "modern Presidency" may date from the post-FDR period, the concept is far older. Each generation has had its version of the modern Presidency, and what is more remarkable is that each version has contained essentially the same elements. The "modern Presidents" of each generation have played a prominent role in setting the legislative agenda and asserting control over the bureaucracy. They have exercised unilateral authority and served as popular symbols of national unity. The Progressives provided the clearest statement of the assumptions underlying the myth of the modern Presidency two decades before Franklin Roosevelt was elected. Abraham Lincoln demonstrated the power and influence of the office on a scale unimagined by most twentieth-century Presidents, and Andrew Jackson showed that a powerful modern Presidency was possible, even necessary, in the context of a limited government. Indeed, it was the first Presidency—the Presidency of George Washington—that was the first to exhibit the elements of the modern Presidency. The modern Presidency was born not in the middle of the twentieth century but at the end of the eighteenth century.

THE PROGRESSIVE PRESIDENCY

One does not have to look very hard to find the elements of the modern Presidency in both the thought and the behavior of the Progressives. Before coming to the Presidency, Woodrow Wilson had developed a theoretical foundation for the practice of the modern Presidency. At the end of the nineteenth century, he identified a dangerous lack of direction in American politics. He spoke of "leaderless government" and the problems it posed for the future of American politics.[1] Initially he believed these difficulties could be overcome by creating a more parliamentary system in which the speaker would take over the role of chief executive and the President would be reduced to a mere administrator.[2] The speaker would supply the legislature, the government, and the nation with the unity and direction it was sorely lacking.

But by 1908, when he wrote *Constitutional Government*, Woodrow Wilson had clearly changed his mind.[3] He had not changed his mind about the need for unity and direction, however. He proclaimed: "There can be no successful government without leadership or without the intimate, almost instinctive, coordination of the organs of life and action."[4] Where Wilson had changed was in his belief that Congress could provide the source of such leadership. Even in *Congressional Government* he had described Congress as

> a collection of men representing each his neighborhood, each his local interest; an alarmingly large proportion of this legislation is "special," all of it is at best only a limping compromise between the conflicting interests of innumerable localities represented.[5]

In 1885 he still held out hope for a transformation of Congress, but by 1908 he had turned from Congress to the Presidency as the most likely source of leadership. Wilson came to believe that:

> Greatly as the practice and influence of Presidents [have] varied, there can be no mistaking the fact that we have grown more and more inclined from generation to generation to look to the President as the unifying force in our complex system, the leader of both his party and the nation.[6]

Wilson believed that the Founders had created a "Newtonian Constitution" that emphasized checks and balances as opposed to growth and

---

1. Woodrow Wilson, "Leaderless Government," in *College and State,* ed. Roy Stannard Baker and William E. Dodd, 2 vols. (New York: Harper Brothers, 1925).
2. Woodrow Wilson, *Congressional Government* (Boston: Houghton Mifflin, 1885).
3. Woodrow Wilson, *Constitutional Government* (New York: Columbia University Press, 1908).
4. Ibid., 57.
5. Wilson, *Congressional Government,* 73.
6. Wilson, *Constitutional Government,* 60.

change. In particular they had created a fairly limited presidential office. But he believed that the office gradually had been transformed by its individual occupants and the variety of circumstances they faced. From George Washington and Thomas Jefferson, to Andrew Jackson, Abraham Lincoln, and Grover Cleveland, Woodrow Wilson saw a possibility of presidential strength not envisioned by the authors of the Constitution.[7]

Wilson was not willing to rest content with the occasional signs of presidential strength. He believed that a more radical and more fundamental change was needed. He no longer believed that a major change in the written Constitution was possible, but he also believed that such a change might be unnecessary. In writing *Constitutional Government,* Wilson sought to transform public opinion. As James Ceaser has explained:

> The "living constitution"—the actual regime as fixed not only by Constitutional provisions, but by opinion and practice—would have to be changed by means of a basic transformation of the public's views under which the people would come to regard the executive as the most legitimate source of political authority.[8]

The original written Constitution would remain, but the government would be transformed through a new concept of legitimacy. In *Constitutional Government* Wilson elaborated this new understanding of government.

Woodrow Wilson clearly envisioned the role of the President as chief legislator. He complained that some previous Presidents had failed to accept this role:

> They have held the strict literary theory of the Constitution, the Whig theory, the Newtonian theory, and have acted as if they thought that Pennsylvania Avenue should have been even longer than it is; that there should be no intimate communication of any kind between the Capitol and the White House; that the President as a man was no more at liberty to lead the Congress by persuasion than he was at liberty as President to dominate them by authority.[9]

But Wilson concluded that "the President is at liberty, both in law and conscience, to be as big a man as he can."[10] Because the executive is in

7. Ibid., 55–59.
8. James W. Ceaser, *Presidential Selection: Theory and Development* (Princeton: Princeton University Press, 1979), 172.
9. Wilson, *Constitutional Government,* 70.
10. Ibid.

daily contact with "practical conditions and exigencies," the legislature should be "very hospitable" to its suggestions:

> A President's messages to Congress have no more weight or authority than their intrinsic reasonableness and importance give them: but that is their only Constitutional limitation. The Constitution certainly does not forbid the President to back them up, as General Washington did, with such personal force and influence as he may possess.[11]

Wilson's argument does at least pay lip service to the Constitution, but popular opinion and not the Constitution would ultimately provide legitimacy for Wilson's revitalized Presidency.[12] The President should play a leadership role because he is the only representative of the nation as a whole. When the President speaks, he "speaks with an authority and a responsibility the people themselves have given him."[13] His position as a unified national leader allows him to impart a sense of direction to the process of legislation that the Congress itself is incapable of providing. Wilson believed that the most successful Presidents of the past had performed such a function, and he was persuaded that "times of stress and change must more and more thrust upon [the President] the attitude of originator of policies."[14] Wilson never seriously considered the possibility that this leadership role was inherent in the Constitution. He saw it as the gradual and fortuitous development of political practice, a development that could best be perpetuated and strengthened by his new theory of government.

Thus Wilson illustrates both the strengths and the weaknesses of the myth of the modern Presidency. He correctly identifies the importance of leadership to the modern Presidency, but he believes that it can be developed only if the President escapes from or transforms the constitutional office.

Woodrow Wilson's view of administration also reflects many of the elements of the "modern Presidency." Wilson neither suggested nor created

11. Ibid., 72–73. This language is similar to that used by Theodore Roosevelt in his "stewardship theory" (see note 25 below).

12. For a discussion of Wilson's use of constitutional rhetoric while trying to transform the Constitution as created by the Framers, see Chris Wolfe, "Woodrow Wilson: Interpreting the Constitution," in *Review of Politics* 41 (January 1979), 121–42; and Charles R. Kesler, "Woodrow Wilson and the Statesmanship of Progress," in *Natural Right and Political Right,* ed. Thomas R. Silver and Peter W. Schramm (Durham, N.C.: Carolina Academic Press, 1984), 115–17.

13. Wilson, *Constitutional Government,* 74.

14. Ibid., 73.

a large bureaucracy within the White House, but he did see that the size and activity of modern American government would require adjustments in the character of administration and the President's relation to his subordinates:

> As the business of the government becomes more complex and extended, . . . the President is becoming more and more political and less and less an executive officer. . . . Only the larger sort of executive questions are brought to him. Departments which run with easy routine . . . may proceed with their business for months and even years without demanding his attention; and no department is in any sense under his direct charge. Cabinet meetings do not discuss detail. . . . If he is indeed the executive, he must act almost entirely by delegation.[15]

Wilson devoted a great deal of attention to the issue of administrative delegation. One of his most influential essays called for a new science of public administration, a science that would ensure the efficient, effective, and neutral implementation of the President's policy.[16]

Ironically, Wilson sought a more neutral administration precisely because he believed it would better serve the political goals of the President. Past Presidents had relied on a politicized bureaucracy to carry out their marching orders, but Wilson saw a problem in such a bureaucracy. It inevitably led to a dispersion of power. By employing party politicians in the administration, the President brought into positions of authority persons with their own political base. But Wilson saw a positive change taking place in which

> our later Presidents have apparently ceased to regard the cabinet as a council of party leaders. . . . They look upon it rather as a body of personal advisers whom the President chooses from the ranks of those whom he personally trusts and prefers to look to for advice.[17]

This ideal cabinet member does not sound all that different from the White House staffer described by the Brownlow Commission in 1937—an apolitical operative with no political aspirations who serves the President alone.[18]

15. Ibid., 66–67.

16. Woodrow Wilson, "The Study of Administration," *Political Science Quarterly* 2 (July 1887), 197–222.

17. Wilson, *Constitutional Government*, 75.

18. *Report of the President's Committee on Administrative Management*, (Washington, D.C.: U.S. Government Printing Office, 1937).

In the area of foreign affairs, Woodrow Wilson saw the greatest potential for the exercise of unilateral powers on the part of the President. Wilson claimed that "the initiative in foreign affairs, which the President possesses without any restriction whatever, is virtually the power to control them absolutely."[19] Wilson might have wanted to qualify this statement in later years, particularly in regard to the treaty-making power. But the central point here is that Wilson anticipated the recent scholarship that has tied the rise of the "modern President's" discretionary power to America's increased role in international politics following World War II. Wilson believed that this aspect of the "modern Presidency" was the inevitable result of the Spanish-American War and the changes that followed.

> The President can never again be the mere domestic figure he has been throughout so large a part of our history. The nation has risen to the first rank in power and resources. . . . Our President must always, henceforth, be one of the greatest powers in the world. . . . We have but begun to see the Presidential office in this light; but it is the light which will more and more beat upon it, and more and more determine its character and its effects upon the politics of the nation.[20]

Wilson perhaps comes closest to the concept of the "modern Presidency" in his understanding of the personal character of the office. He said, "It is easier to write of the President than of the Presidency."[21] It was not the office but rather its occupants who had given life to the organs of government. The President should be:

> A man who will be and who will seem to the country . . . an embodiment of the character and purpose it wishes its government to have—a man who understands his own day and the needs of the country, and who has the personality and the initiative to enforce his views both upon the people and upon Congress.[22]

The President was to serve as an embodiment of the nation, a personal symbol of nationhood:

> The nation as a whole has chosen him, and is conscious that it has no other political spokesman. His is the only national voice in af-

19. Wilson, *Constitutional Government*, 77.
20. Ibid., 78.
21. Ibid., 57.
22. Ibid., 65.

fairs. Let him once win the admiration and confidence of the country, and no other single force can withstand him, no combination of forces can easily overpower him. His position takes the imagination of the country. He is the representative of no constituency, but of the whole people. When he speaks in his true character, he speaks for no special interest. If he rightly interpret the national thought and boldly insist upon it, he is irresistible; and the country never feels the zest of action so much as when its President is of such insight and calibre. Its instinct is for unified action, and it craves a single leader. It is for this reason that it will often prefer to choose a man rather than a party. A President whom it trusts can not only lead it, but form it to his own views.[23]

This personal relationship between the President and the nation had been the key to presidential power in the past and would remain so in the future. Because this relationship was the primary source of presidential power and therefore of national unity, Woodrow Wilson believed it was necessary to strengthen it in any way possible. To that end, he sought to change the system of presidential selection from one dominated by parties and party leaders to one controlled by candidates and the people. Wilson had as little use for the existing political parties as he did for the Founders' Constitution. Intermediate institutions such as parties diffused power. Nomination of presidential candidates by party conventions interposed party leaders between the people and the candidate. The candidate in such a system turned out to be a compromise among competing interests rather than a spokesperson for the national interest.[24]

The presidential primary was consistently championed by Wilson as a way to circumvent the party organization and tie the candidate directly to the people of the nation. In 1912 Wilson went so far as to propose a direct national primary that would have eliminated any role for party leaders in the selection of the President. A President chosen through such a system would not be bound by any special interests or any party bosses. He would be free to pursue his view of the national interest presented in the campaign and ratified by his popular selection. The foot soldiers and lieutenants of the party would be pushed to the side, leaving room for the unfettered heroism of a single leader.

Although we have spoken mainly of Wilson the scholar rather than Wilson the President, there can be little doubt that these views informed his

23. Ibid., 68.

24. For a discussion of the tension between Wilson's identification with the party government school and his desire for candidate-centered parties, see Ceaser, *Presidential Selection*, 197–207.

Presidency. But if we want to find in the Progressive era the deeds of the modern Presidency, rather than just the words, we do not have to wait for the Presidency of Woodrow Wilson. The model of the Progressive Presidency, and in many respects the modern Presidency is found in Theodore Roosevelt.

Theodore Roosevelt does provide a succinct theoretical defense of unilateral presidential action in his "stewardship theory." According to him, the President is free to act in the public interest in any way he sees fit as long as there is no precise legal prohibition of such action. What the Constitution and the laws do not prohibit, they allow.[25]

It was, however, Theodore Roosevelt's political practice even more than his political theories that helped to shape the modern Presidency. He called together business and labor leaders to "persuade" them to settle the anthracite coal strike. He created federal bird sanctuaries by executive order. He used foreign policy to enhance unilateral presidential powers, sending troops to the Philippines without prior congressional approval, he quietly supported the rebellion that made the Panama Canal possible, and he mediated the Russo-Japanese War.

Theodore Roosevelt also took seriously the role of legislative leader. Even though he assumed the Presidency following an assassination, and pledging a continuity of policy, it did not take him long to establish his own legislative agenda. From environmental legislation to trust regulation and railroad reform, Theodore Roosevelt saw himself as an initiator of legislation. He not only made proposals, but also worked continuously to ensure their passage, seeking votes among Democrats as well as Republicans, creating and abandoning coalitions in order to obtain a legislative majority. The Hepburn Act regulating railroad rates may be the greatest tribute to Roosevelt's legislative skill, but it is far from the only example. Theodore Roosevelt was no idle observer of the legislative process.

It is significant that, before becoming President, Theodore Roosevelt had served as a Civil Service Commissioner and as President of the New York City Police Board. In both positions he had championed the cause of administrative reform. He reacted against the corruption of administration through the spoils system and the urban political machines, but his concern was not only with the ethical problem of corruption but also with the political problems it caused. Corruption prevented the efficient implementation of policy and undercut effective political leadership. As President of the New York Police Board, Theodore Roosevelt undertook the strict enforcement of the Sunday saloon closing laws, in opposition to

25. For a complete statement of the stewardship theory, see *The Autobiography of Theodore Roosevelt*, ed. Wayne Andrews (New York: Scribner's, 1958), 197–200.

the established practice of looking the other way. The reasons for this "crusade" have often been misunderstood. Roosevelt was not particularly sympathetic to prohibitionist sentiment, nor was he hostile to the ethnic voters who were most opposed to Sunday closing laws. He merely thought that the principle of enforcing established laws and policies must be upheld. The limited selective enforcement of the laws was inconsistent with governmental integrity and control of government policy by responsible elected officials. The established laws and policies of the government must not be thwarted by administrative subordinates or the unelected party machine.[26]

Although there have been some complaints that Theodore Roosevelt was all too willing to use political patronage to enhance his political fortunes once in the White House, he remained a friend of administrative reform. His ultimate goal was to make the administration of government responsive to the public interest. In 1905 he appointed the Keep Commission, which was charged with investigating the management of the federal government. He broadened the use and justification of independent regulatory commissions, and through his personal secretary George Cortelyou, Theodore Roosevelt began to establish more-rigorous bureaucratic procedures to handle the flow of information within the White House offices. He understood that such political control was essential to an effective modern Presidency.

Theodore Roosevelt is also a model of the popular personal President. Although he remained a loyal Republican until 1912, and even offended many reformers by his support of Blaine's candidacy in 1884, his main source of political strength flowed from his popular following and not from the party leadership. He was nominated to the Vice-Presidency because of his heroic exploits in the Spanish-American War and because the party organization in New York preferred to kick this potentially dangerous maverick upstairs and out of state. Roosevelt cultivated the image of the individual hero fighting various forms of corruption and injustice. He stamped the Presidency with his personality. The image of teeth and glasses, the Teddy bear, the exploits of the frontiersman, the charge up San Juan Hill, and the father rollicking with his children all became important elements of the mythology surrounding him. Through this mythology, Theodore Roosevelt personalized the office and served as a symbol of the American character.[27]

26. For a discussion of Roosevelt's enforcement of the Sunday closing laws, see Edmund Morris, *Rise of Theodore Roosevelt* (New York: Coward, McCann & Geoghegan, 1979), 496–504.

27. For a more extended discussion of Theodore Roosevelt's Presidency, see Morris, *Rise of Theodore Roosevelt;* William H. Harbaugh, *The Life and Times of Theodore Roosevelt*

THE NINETEENTH-CENTURY PRESIDENCY

Theodore Roosevelt himself often looked back to an earlier Presidency to find a model of an active modern President. He looked to Abraham Lincoln. Lincoln was actively engaged throughout his Presidency in an attempt to balance the antiwar and abolitionist factions in Congress and in the public at large. The more we learn of Lincoln, the more we are struck by his skill at using different factions in the legislature to promote his policies at different times. Often he appeared to be pushed by the legislature to a particular course of action, but on closer inspection it is obvious that Lincoln orchestrated the legislative agenda throughout his Presidency.[28] This is not to suggest that Lincoln was actively concerned with the details of every piece of legislation before Congress. What it means is that Lincoln exercised active legislative leadership in regard to the most important issues of the day.

It is less clear that Lincoln's Presidency can be associated with the administrative developments of the modern Presidency. His cabinet reflected the political representation of various factions of the party and not the apolitical professionals recommended by Woodrow Wilson. Nonetheless, the tremendous growth in the size of government resulting from the war put the President at the center of a large modern bureaucracy. It is also striking that Lincoln's secretaries John Hay and John Nicolay were the first to achieve distinction as official personal aides to the President. Perhaps having picked his cabinet in order to balance competing political concerns, Lincoln saw the need to have administrative assistants in the White House that were loyal to him alone.

If there is any doubt regarding Lincoln's relationship to the modern administrative Presidency, there can be none regarding Lincoln's willingness to use unilateral presidential powers. Even Franklin Roosevelt might blush at Lincoln's independent exercise of authority. From his suspension

---

(New York: Oxford University Press, 1975); John Morton Blum, *The Republican Roosevelt* (Cambridge, Mass.: Harvard University Press, 1954); and Lewis L. Gould, *The Presidency of Theodore Roosevelt* (Lawrence: University of Kansas Press, 1991).

28. Harry T. Williams depicts a conservative Lincoln using his political skills to moderate the radicals (*Lincoln and the Radicals* [Madison: University of Wisconsin Press, 1941]). More-recent historians have spoken of Lincoln's political attempts to placate conservatives while pursuing a more radical agenda. See, for example, Stephen B. Oates, "Republican in the White House," in *Abraham Lincoln and the American Political Tradition*, ed. John L. Thomas (Amherst: University of Massachusetts Press, 1986), 98–110; Don E. Fehrenbacher, *Lincoln in Text and Context* (Stanford, Calif.: Stanford University Press, 1987), esp. 108–9; and James M. McPherson, "The Hedgehog and the Foxes," in his *Abraham Lincoln and the Second American Revolution* (New York: Oxford University Press, 1990), 113–30.

of the writ of habeas corpus, to his arrest of members of the Maryland legislature to prevent them from voting for secession, to his issuance of the Emancipation Proclamation, no President before or since has better demonstrated the potential of the office for unilateral action.

As heroic symbol of the nation, all other Presidents must take a back seat to Lincoln. To a great extent the heroics of earlier Presidents occurred before they came to office. Washington led the colonists to victory in the Revolutionary War, Jefferson wrote the Declaration of Independence, and Jackson was a military hero in battles against the British, the Spanish, and Native Americans. Lincoln moved beyond the possibility of the hero President to demonstrate the possibility of the heroic Presidency. By defining and articulating the principles of union, Lincoln became the preeminent symbol of that union. He captured the ambiguity and complexity of popular sentiment, giving due weight to the legal restraints and compromises that the abolitionists would have ignored, while at the same time appealing to the principles of liberty and equality that would ultimately come into conflict with slavery. His personal sense of law and justice gave meaning and legitimacy to the cause of union. With Lincoln the office of the Presidency was personalized, and it is his personality that has haunted and invigorated all subsequent Presidencies.

JACKSON AND THE MODERN PRESIDENCY

Even if Lincoln may legitimately claim to be the greatest modern President, he is not entitled to be called the first. Robert Remini made an extensive case for the claim that it was Andrew Jackson who radically transformed the office of the Presidency. According to Remini:

> The fight that ensued between the President and Congress [during Jackson's administration] profoundly changed the relationship between the executive and legislative branches. The operation of government as originally conceived by the Founding Fathers, with its delicate system of checks and balances and its dependence on the supremacy of Congress in originating laws, was altered to such an extent that Henry Clay called it a "revolution . . . tending towards a total change of the . . . character of the Government."[29]

29. Robert Remini, *The Revolutionary Age of Andrew Jackson* (New York: Harper & Row, 1976), 123–24.

In one important respect, however, Jackson does not fit the picture of the modern Presidency. Although Jackson believed in an activist Presidency, and in the maintenance and expansion of the union, much of his Presidency was devoted to checking the growth in the power of the national government in domestic affairs.

We have tended to associate activist Presidencies with a commitment to more activist government, but that is a mistake. The two do not inevitably go together, as Jackson's Presidency illustrates. A powerful, active President can be primarily concerned with maintaining the limits of limited government.

Clearly this is the case with regard to legislative affairs. The veto power is the President's most obvious weapon in battles with the legislature, and it is not surprising that Jackson was known for his use of the veto. Jackson had a legislative agenda, but it was one that could be pursued primarily through his use and threat to use the veto. His goal was to prevent rather than promote government action. In his veto of the Bank Bill, Remini claims, Jackson transformed the character of the presidential veto from a device to be used only as a protection against unconstitutional legislation to a presidential tool of policy. Only nine vetoes had been exercised by Presidents in the first forty years of the Presidency, and only three of these vetoes dealt with major pieces of legislation. Jackson, however, used the veto a total of twelve times during his eight years in office. More important than the number, according to Remini, was the fact that Jackson used the veto to defend his policy preferences.

By claiming the right to veto legislation for policy reasons, Jackson insinuated the executive into the legislative process. Now "Congress must carefully consider the President's wishes on all legislation before enacting it, or risk a veto." Remini concludes that this interpretation of the veto altered

> the basic equality between the branches of government as written into the Constitution by the Founding Fathers. Instead of a 50-50 relationship between the chief executive and Congress, it would become a 67-33 relationship in the President's favor.[30]

Webster compared Jackson's action with those of James II of England "a month before he was compelled to fly the kingdom."[31] He contended that it "denies to the judiciary the interpretation of the laws, and claims to

---

30. Ibid., 135.
31. "Veto of the Bank Bill," in *The Papers of Daniel Webster: Speeches and Formal Writings*, vol. 1, ed. Charles Wiltse (Hanover, N.H.: University Press of New England, 1986), 517.

divide with Congress the power of originating statutes."[32] Jackson thus sought to make the President the chief legislator of the nation.

Jackson transformed the idea of administration, but that transformation is not usually associated with the idea of the modern administrative state. Jacksonian administration is synonymous with the spoils system, the domination of administration by partisan political concerns. What is too often forgotten is that the spoils system was itself an administrative reform. The spoils system was a reaction against the doctrine of "property in office" under which an administrative official was seen to have what amounted to a property right in his office for as long as he did not break the law or demonstrate overwhelming incompetence.

Jackson claimed, however, that this idea was inconsistent with democratic values. It led to the creation of a separate governing class that served its own interests rather than the interests of the people. It limited the people's participation in government. And, most important of all, it created an institutional obstacle to the implementation of the President's program. The elected representative of the people could be thwarted by an unelected elite. By introducing the spoils system, Jackson sought to enhance the ability of the President to pursue and implement the policies that were ratified by his election.

The corruption of the spoils system may have been inevitable, just as it may have been inevitable that the spoils system would enhance the power of party leaders at the expense of the independent power of the President. But for Jackson the spoils system was a reform that supported the modern Presidency. In many respects Jackson's spoils system anticipates the concerns that have given rise to the growth of the White House staff, specifically that the President needs loyal administrative aides. And Jackson's administrative reform was not limited to the adoption of the spoils system. According to Matthew Crenson, Jacksonian administration also exhibited many of the traits of advanced bureaucratic systems.[33] Jackson created a complex system of hierarchical authority and responsibility that gives him claim to the title of the first modern administrative Presidency.

Jackson is also identified with the unilateral use of presidential authority. He removed his Secretary of the Treasury William Duane without the approval of the Senate. He removed the deposits of the government from the Bank of the United States without congressional approval, and in fact in opposition to a resolution passed by the House of Representatives attesting to the safety of the deposits in the Bank. Both removals are based

32. "Veto of the Bank Bill" in *The Age of Jackson*, ed. Robert Remini (Columbia: University of South Carolina Press, 1972), 528.

33. Matthew A. Crenson, *The Federal Machine: Beginnings of Bureaucracy in Jacksonian America* (Baltimore: Johns Hopkins University Press, 1975), 104–39.

on a single premise: The President has a right to act unilaterally. As Jackson argued in his "Protest":

> Thus it was settled by the Constitution, the laws, and the whole practice of the government that the entire executive power is vested in the President of the United States; that as incident to that power [is] the right of appointing and removing those officers who are to aid him in the execution of the laws . . . ; that the custody of the public property and money is an executive function which . . . has always been exercised through the Secretary of the Treasury and his subordinates; that in the performance of his duties he is subject to the supervision and control of the President. . . .[34]

Remini argues that the doctrine as expressed by Jackson was quite radical. Congress had traditionally been understood to control the purse strings of government. Congress had authorized the Secretary of the Treasury to remove the government's funds, but the Secretary was to report to the Congress if he took any such action. Moreover, the power was given to the Treasury Secretary and not to the President. In ordering the removal, Jackson "assumed control of public funds."[35]

The right to remove cabinet officials was also open to question. In *Federalist* No. 77 Hamilton had said that the Senate would participate in removal as well as appointment.[36] Although in the first Congress Madison had successfully defended the doctrine of presidential removal, the doctrine had never been fully tested. Presidents had previously solved any problems in the cabinet by getting cabinet members to resign.[37] Jackson, unable to obtain Duane's resignation, was forced to address the issue directly and claimed that removal was an absolute prerogative of the President.

Congressional interference in removal or in the execution of presidential instructions regarding the custody of government funds was, according to Jackson, an unjustified interference in the exercise of executive power.[38] In the mind of the Whigs, executive discretion had replaced the rule of law as the basis of American government. In any event, Jackson provided ample precedents for the unilateral authority of the modern Presidency.

34. "Jackson's 'Protest,'" in Remini, ed., *The Age of Jackson*, 114.
35. Ibid., 155.
36. Alexander Hamilton et al., *The Federalist*, ed. Jacob E. Cooke (Cleveland: Meridian Books, 1961), 515.
37. Remini, *The Revolutionary Age of Andrew Jackson*, 155.
38. "Protest," in James D. Richardson, *A Compilation of the Messages and Papers of the Presidents*, 20 vols. (New York: Bureau of National Literature, 1897), 3:1305.

Jackson is also often credited with creating the mass-based political campaign that is in turn the source of the modern popular Presidency.[39] Perhaps more than in any presidential election before or since, the election of 1832 was a referendum on a particular political issue: Jackson's opposition to the Second Bank of the United States. Jackson's victory encouraged him to believe that the nation accepted his vision of democracy. In a meeting with his cabinet after the election, Jackson claimed that his reelection was "a decision of the people against the bank" and stated that it was now his intention to "carry into effect their decision."[40] Thus Jackson justified his decision to remove the funds of the government from the Bank. The removal would carry into effect, through the office of the Presidency, the decision of the people against the Bank.

Jackson reiterated this claim in his "Protest" message: "The President is the direct representative of the American people, . . . elected by the people and responsible to them."[41] In this view Jackson did not derive his powers from Congress or the laws. He acted by virtue of a mandate granted to him by the people, and he was responsible to them alone for his actions.

As Remini explains, "the entire tone of the 'Protest' constituted a dangerous challenge to the traditional theory of legislative government."[42] Daniel Webster complained in response to the "Protest":

> The Constitution nowhere calls [the President] the representative of the American people. It could not do so with the least propriety. He is not chosen directly by the people, but by a body of electors. . . . If he may be allowed to consider himself as the sole representative of all of the American people . . . then I say sir that the government (I will not say the people) has already a master.[43]

39. Tulis notes that even Jackson did not personally engage in popular rhetoric, but he did use his Annual Message to Congress, his Nullification Proclamation, his Protest to Congress, and a partisan press to influence popular opinion. (Jeffrey K. Tulis, *The Rhetorical Presidency* [Princeton: Princeton University Press, 1897], 73–75). Tulis emphasizes the indirect character of Jackson's communications with the people, and it is true that popular leadership generally took a different form in the nineteenth century than in the twentieth. That difference in form, however, may reflect a more general difference in standards of public decorum rather than a qualitative change in the office. It may also reflect the limits of communication and transportation technology. Jackson relied on the partisan press because it was the most effective means available for reaching the people. But given the opportunity, it is difficult to imagine that Jackson would not have used a medium, such as television, that would have allowed him to speak directly to the people.

40. "Removal of Public Deposits," in Remini, ed., *The Age of Jackson*, 101.

41. "Protest," in Richardson, *Compilation*, 3:1309.

42. Remini, *The Revolutionary Age of Andrew Jackson*, 165.

43. "Webster's Reply to the 'Protest,'" in Remini, ed., *The Age of Jackson*, 120–21.

According to Remini, Webster was absolutely correct in his assessment of the situation:

> Previous Presidents had understood and appreciated that the seat of government was the Congress, and . . . they had functioned like prime ministers. . . . Jackson, on the other hand, now claimed he was the head of the entire government and the spokesman of the American people.[44]

Jackson clearly saw the President as the tribune of the people. According to Remini, this point more than any other indicates the transformation of the presidential office. But it is not the only example of Jackson assuming the functions of the modern Presidency. From his active participation in the legislative process, to his control over administration, and most of all in his popular leadership, it is obvious that Jackson possessed the attributes most often associated with the modern Presidency.

But perhaps the transformation of the office was not as great as either Remini or Jackson's Whig opponents believed. Ironically, Remini's view that Jackson was the first modern President rests on the Whig assumption that the Constitution created a weak presidential office. But it is possible that Remini finds the elements of the modern Presidency in Jackson's Presidency not because Jackson transformed the office but because he recognized the potentials of the constitutional Presidency.

THE FIRST MODERN PRESIDENT

If the Constitution created the modern Presidency, we should be able to identify the elements of the modern Presidency even earlier in our history than Jackson's Presidency. Could it be, in fact, that the elements of the modern Presidency can be found as far back as the first Presidency, the Presidency of George Washington? It has become accepted folk wisdom that the office of President was created for Washington. Few doubted that he would be its first occupant, and many of the fears of a strong Presidency were allayed by that fact. What is equally important is the extent to which Washington's Presidency served to fill in the outlines of the Presidency found in the Constitution and to give life to the Presidency. Wash-

44. Remini, *The Revolutionary Age of Andrew Jackson*, 167.

ington's actions as the first chief executive were directed precisely to the areas that Greenstein associates with the modern Presidency.[45]

From the beginning, Washington took an active role in the legislative process. Through his Secretary of the Treasury, Alexander Hamilton, the Washington administration immediately sketched out a legislative agenda and began to lobby for its passage. The first Congress had to design the substructure of the government itself, and Washington and Hamilton were actively involved in this process. The most controversial legislative issue of the day was funding of the war debt. Here too Washington and Hamilton led the way, engineering a remarkable legislative victory. Hamilton was less successful with his report on manufactures, but the point is not that the administration was always successful but that it had and pursued a legislative agenda. Washington established a precedent that the President would be actively engaged in legislative questions.

The size and shape of the modern executive branch were determined during Washington's Presidency. The cabinet departments were created, and, more important, the relationship between the President and the executive branch began to take shape. It was in Washington's administration that the issue of the removal power first arose, and was decided in favor of the President. Unless the President had the power to remove executive branch officials, he could not be held accountable for the conduct of the executive branch. This principle helped to establish the idea of an independent executive branch under the direction of Washington. In addition, it was Washington who first defended the idea of executive privilege as a necessary support for the integrity and independence of the executive branch.

The question of unilateral presidential powers was most obvious in the debate over Washington's proclamation of neutrality. Without prior congressional approval, Washington issued his proclamation stating that the United States remained neutral in the conflict between Britain and France. In one sense this would not appear to be a radical assertion of authority. As Hamilton pointed out, Washington was only stating the obvious. No congressional declaration of war had been issued, so hostilities toward neither side had been officially authorized.

But in a broader sense Washington was staking a claim to a major source of unilateral authority. Through his proclamation he was unilaterally in-

---

45. For a more extensive account of the Washington Presidency, see James T. Flexner, *George Washington and the New Nation, 1783–1793* (Boston: Little, Brown & Co., 1970); and James T. Flexner, *George Washington: Anguish and Farewell, 1793–1799* (Boston: Little, Brown & Co., 1972). The only single volume devoted to Washington's Presidency is Forrest McDonald, *The Presidency of George Washington* (Lawrence: University of Kansas Press, 1974).

terpreting the U.S. treaty with France by deciding that it created no presumption of support for the French in their fight. Moreover, Washington was making policy. Congress had clearly not decided whether to act or on which side. By proclaiming neutrality in the midst of the policy debate in Congress, Washington created an overwhelming presumption in favor of inaction. Congress was incensed that Washington was exercising unilateral authority in foreign-policy-making, but it was not able to counteract his policy. Thus it was our first President who demonstrated the potential for the unilateral exercise of presidential power.

Was the aloof Washington in any way a model of the modern personal President? We may find it hard to imagine Washington in the midst of a modern democratic political campaign. Nonetheless, with the exception of Lincoln, no other Presidency was as dependent on personality as Washington's. As we have already mentioned, many thought the office was designed for Washington. The father of his country, the man who had led the nation to victory and independence, was the quintessential heroic President. The trust and adoration for Washington allowed him to maintain popular support in the face of some of the most divisive issues the nation would face. By force of personality and character he was able to serve as a symbol of unity, a symbol that helped to support government while its institutions grew and took root.

Washington never lost sight of the role he personally played in cementing the union and creating respect for the national government. He was always conscious of the precedents he was setting for future Presidents and future generations. In spite of the difficulties of travel, he toured the new nation in order to create a personal attachment between the people and the national government. He knew that he presented the embodiment of the Presidency and the nation. The identity of the Presidency and the nation was intertwined with the person of Washington to an extent that surpasses any twentieth-century Presidency. If the recent "discovery" of the "personal Presidency" would not lead Washington to uproarious laughter, it would certainly bring an ironic smile to his face.

THE ORIGINS OF THE MODERN PRESIDENCY

There is always the exception that proves the rule, but the number of exceptions to the rule that traces the modern Presidency to Franklin Roosevelt are too numerous to be ignored. Would Washington, Jackson, Lincoln, Theodore Roosevelt, or Wilson feel at home in the presidential office of 1991? In some respects, no. It is too large—there are too many people, too many issues, perhaps even too much responsibility. But after their initial shock over the size and complexity of the government and the nation, they would be likely to say, "The more things change, the more they stay the same." In his relationship with the legislature, in his relationship to the executive branch, in his need to exercise unilateral authority, and in his unique relationship with the people, the potential and the problems of the President remain relatively constant.

We have only scratched the surface in identifying the elements of the modern Presidency in the period before Franklin Roosevelt. Biographers and other scholars have written volumes explaining how Washington, Jackson, Lincoln, Theodore Roosevelt, and Wilson transformed the office of the Presidency. We have not even touched on the claims of the biographers of William McKinley, Grover Cleveland, James Polk, and Thomas Jefferson.[46] Each of these Presidents did make important contributions in refining the office, but in defining the office it is the Constitution, more than any particular President, that has had the greatest impact.

Greenstein's definition of the elements of the modern Presidency is largely accurate. It is also true that Franklin Roosevelt made unique contributions in each of these areas. But as we have seen, so have virtually all our great and near-great Presidents. The reason for this is that the potential for the modern Presidency was created not by Franklin Roosevelt but by the Constitution. It was the Constitution that gave the President a major role in the legislative process. It is the Constitution that directs the President to the problems and potential of administrative control. It is the Constitution that lays the groundwork for the exercise of independent unilateral executive authority. And it is the Constitution that creates the personal dynamic between the people and the President.

We have lost sight of this because we have lost sight of the Constitution. The Constitution is a living document in that it gives rise to a number of different manifestations. Not all Presidents or all Presidencies look the same. The potential may remain constant, but the actualization of the potential is highly variable, depending on circumstances and personality. But the Constitution has yet to be overwhelmed by personality or events. It

46. The series on the American Presidency being edited by the University of Kansas Press is particularly useful in showing the elements of the modern Presidency in pre-FDR Presidencies. See, for example, Lewis L. Gould, *The Presidency of William McKinley* (Lawrence: University of Kansas Press, 1980); Richard E. Welch, *The Presidencies of Grover Cleveland* (Lawrence: University of Kansas Press, 1988); Paul H. Bergeron, *The Presidency of James K. Polk* (Lawrence: University of Kansas Press, 1987); and Forrest McDonald, *The Presidency of Thomas Jefferson* (Lawrence: University of Kansas Press, 1976). Robert M. Johnstone Jr., *Jefferson and the Presidency: Leadership in the Young Republic* (Ithaca, N.Y.: Cornell University Press, 1978), also points to a number of parallels between the Jeffersonian Presidency and the modern Presidency.

is more our political scholarship than our political practice that has been overwhelmed by changing events and the changing personalities that have occupied the constitutional office. Scholars have interpreted the Constitution in light of their likes and dislikes of particular Presidents. They have used the Constitution as a weapon or scapegoat to support their political preferences. Ultimately, they have come to ignore it as they have been overwhelmed by personalities and events. If we can recover the constitutional Presidency, however, we may be able to recover a perspective that will allow us a more complete and more lasting perspective within which to view the American Presidency and American government.

CHAPTER TWO

The Constitutional Presidency

To recover an appreciation of the constitutional Presidency, we must first escape the perspective on the Constitution created by much twentieth-century scholarship. The modern Presidency literature and the scholarship of the Progressives have given us a stilted picture of the constitutional Presidency. As we have seen, the Progressives portrayed the Constitution as an impediment to the development of a powerful modern Presidency. The defense of the constitutional Presidency has fallen primarily to those who want to check the growth of presidential power. William Howard Taft, during the Progressive era, and Edwin Corwin in response to Franklin Roosevelt and the modern Presidency, are notable examples.[1] Both turned to the Constitution as a source of limitations on the powers of the government in general and of the Presidency in particular.

In more recent times Arthur Schlesinger Jr. and Raoul Berger have used the Constitution in opposition to Lyndon Johnson, Richard Nixon, and the imperial Presidency.[2] Both attacked the doctrines of extensive presidential war powers and executive privilege as attempts to invoke nonconstitutional doctrines of prerogative. This restraintist view has come to play an important role in the contemporary constitutional debate; there is a general fear of the dangers of an unrestrained popular Presidency, and the Constitution is seen as the major obstacle to an unrestrained Presidency.

1. Edward S. Corwin, *The President: Office and Powers* (New York: New York University Press, 1940); William Howard Taft, *Our Chief Magistrate and His Powers* (New York: Columbia University Press, 1916).
2. Arthur M. Schlesinger Jr., *The Imperial Presidency* (New York: Popular Library, 1973); Raoul Berger, *Executive Privilege: A Constitutional Myth* (Cambridge, Mass.: Harvard University Press, 1974).

The contemporary constitutional debate generally reflects an oscillation between the Progressive and the restraintist views. Both the Progressive view and the restraintist view, however, are based on a common assumption. They share the belief that the constitutional Presidency is a weak Presidency. The Progressives see this as a problem to be overcome, whereas the restraintists see it as the major safeguard to liberty. But both agree that the President finds little of his power within the Constitution.

In recent years this assumption has been questioned in the work of political scientists such as James Ceaser and the students of Herbert Storing.[3] This third school claims that the authors of the Constitution intentionally established a strong constitutional Presidency. It begins with the assumption that the framers of the Constitution believed that even a limited government must be an effective government.

In the aftermath of the Revolution, the Founders had to determine what form of government would replace the British Parliament and king as the national political authority. The weak central authority under the Articles of Confederation initially appeared to be the solution most consistent with the liberal principles of the Revolution, but Americans soon saw that the Articles could not guarantee internal liberty or external security. The fear of the power of the British government had led to the Revolution, but the fear of the weakness of government under the Articles led to the Constitutional Convention. The Articles were quickly rejected by the Convention, and almost coincident with that rejection was the acceptance of the need for an independent executive authority.

According to this strong constitutional Presidency school, the Constitution sought ways to provide institutional supports for the exercise of political authority in general and executive power in particular. Institutional supports would insulate political authority from direct democracy's tendencies toward shortsightedness, instability, and majority tyranny. The Founders wanted to create a democracy that could effectively exercise political authority and therefore be capable of maintaining itself.

This third school has done much to place the constitutional Presidency in the proper perspective. It recognizes that the Constitution created a role for the President in directing the administration of government, in exercising unilateral authority, and perhaps even in legislative leadership. The constitutional Presidency was born not out of the Revolutionary fear of King George but out of a practical recognition of the problem of maintaining liberal government.

This book grows out of the strong constitutional Presidency school and

3. See, for example, the collection of essays edited by Joseph M. Bessette and Jeffrey Tulis, *The Presidency in the Constitutional Order* (Baton Rouge: Louisiana State University Press, 1981); James W. Ceaser, *Presidential Selection: Theory and Development* (Princeton: Princeton University Press, 1979).

is much indebted to it. But there may also be a limitation in this approach—it may fail to recognize the extent to which the Founders relied on popular opinion, not only as a check on presidential authority but, more important, as a source of presidential authority. In this respect the third school also accepts a part of the myth of the modern Presidency. It accepts the belief that the President's popular leadership role is extra-constitutional. But we shall see that several elements of the constitutional Presidency were created specifically to enhance the President's role as popular leader. For that reason, a fourth view is needed, a view that recognizes both the institutional and the popular sources of presidential authority created by the Constitution, as well as the sources of restraint on the exercise of presidential power. This view will most easily emerge from a careful examination of Article II of the Constitution.

Some will complain that the Constitution tells us little about the Presidency, and furthermore that what it does tell us is ambiguous or contradictory. I shall show, however, the provisions and structure of the Constitution tell us a great deal about the constitutional and the contemporary Presidency. There is a logic to the idea of executive power expressed in the Constitution, a logic that emerges primarily from reading the text of the document, but also from an examination of the debates surrounding the creation and adoption of the Constitution.[4] The implications of the logic may not have been seen in every case by the authors and ratifiers of the Constitution. The Founders gave birth to the Presidency through Article II of the Constitution, but like most parents they may not have understood completely the potential of their progeny.

My argument does not imply, however, that the Constitution is so open-ended that it allows any kind of interpretation. The Constitution has integrity. The Constitution as a whole is what was approved by the Constitutional Convention and later ratified, and what has governed successfully for two centuries. The principles may require elaboration, but elaboration is legitimate only to the extent that it fits well within the context of the document. Interpretation must lead us to a better understanding of the whole, or else it is distortion and not interpretation.

This method of interpretation is best understood in operation. I propose to look at the provisions of Article II of the Constitution to see what the Constitution says, to try to understand the terms of the debate that gave rise to those provisions, and finally to attempt to articulate the logic that animates and gives integrity to the constitutional Presidency.

At the Constitutional Convention there were two identifiable, if not

---

4. For a good discussion of the primacy of the text in constitutional interpretation, see Leslie Friedman Goldstein, *In Defense of the Text: Democracy and Constitutional Theory* (Savage, Md.: Rowman & Littlefield, 1991).

always distinct, strains of thought regarding the sources of a powerful and independent executive. One strain, exemplified by Alexander Hamilton's June 18 speech, links a powerful executive with institutional barriers to popular influence.[5] The other, found in the arguments presented by James Wilson at the Convention, sees presidential authority as a direct outgrowth of popular support.[6] The constitutional Presidency is a product of the combination of these two strains of thought—a combination that is most evident in the language of the Constitution created by Gouverneur Morris.

As we examine the provisions of Article II of the Constitution, we shall see a President who is clearly tied to popular sources of authority but who also has institutional powers that allow for the exercise of discretionary authority. We shall also see the emergence of a new kind of power in Section 3 of Article II. It is not simply power, but influence born of the President's constitutional position and popular national election. Taken together, the popular authority, institutional powers, and political influence provided for in the constitutional office of the Presidency explain much of the development and the contemporary practice of the modern Presidency.

The constitutional Presidency, as we shall see, represents the fulfillment and further refinement of the early modern liberal idea of executive power. The Constitution provides for a powerful and independent executive growing out of and dedicated to the principles of liberal government. But it also represents an advance over previous theories. The written Constitution provides more clearly for the security of both the rights of the people and the powers of the executive. In addition, popular election reduces the conflict between executive power and liberal government, and it may even serve to energize the exercise of executive power. Finally, it demonstrates that political influence may be as important as the power to command in a modern liberal political system.

ARTICLE II, SECTION 1

The executive Power shall be vested in a President of the United States of America. He shall hold his Office during the Term of four

5. *The Records of the Federal Convention of 1787*, 4 vols., ed. Max Farrand (New Haven: Yale University Press, 1966), 1:282–93, 304–11.

6. See, for example, Wilson's comments on June 1 (ibid., 69), where he calls for popular election of the President, arguing that it is necessary to ground the President as well as the legislature on popular consent in order to ensure executive independence.

Years, and, together with the Vice President, chosen for the same Term, be elected, as follows:

Each State shall appoint, in such Manner as the Legislature thereof may direct, a Number of Electors, equal to the whole Number of Senators and Representatives to which the State may be entitled in the Congress; but no Senator or Representative, or Person holding an Office of Trust or Profit under the United States, shall be appointed an Elector.

The Electors shall meet in their respective States, and vote by Ballot for two Persons, of whom one at least shall not be an Inhabitant of the same State with themselves. And they shall make a List of all the Persons voted for, and of the Number of Votes for each; which List they shall sign and certify, and transmit sealed to the Seat of Government of the United States, directed to the President of the Senate. The President of the Senate shall, in the Presence of the Senate and the House of Representatives, open all Certificates, and the Votes shall then be counted. The Person having the greatest Number of Votes shall be the President, if such Number be a majority of the whole Number of Electors appointed; and if there be more than one who have such Majority, and have an equal Number of Votes, then the House of Representatives shall immediately chuse by Ballot one of them for President; and if no Person have a Majority, then from the five highest on the List the said House shall in like Manner chuse the President. But in chusing the President, the Votes shall be taken by States; the Representation from each State having one Vote; A quorum for this Purpose shall consist of a Member or Members from two thirds of the States, and a majority of all the States shall be necessary to a Choice. In every Case, after the Choice of the President, the Person having the greater Number of Votes of the Electors shall be Vice President. But if there should remain two or more who have equal Votes, the Senate shall chuse from them by Ballot the Vice President.

The Congress may determine the Time of chusing the Electors, and the Day on which they shall give their Votes; which Day shall be the same throughout the United States.

No person except a natural born Citizen, or a Citizen of the United States at the time of the Adoption of this Constitution, shall be eligible to the Office of President; neither shall any Person be eligible to that Office who shall not have attained the Age of thirty five Years, and been fourteen Years a Resident within the United States.

In the case of the removal of the President from Office, or of his

Death, Resignation or Inability to discharge the Powers and Duties of the said Office, the Same shall devolve on the Vice President, and the Congress may by law provide for the case of Removal, Death, Resignation, or Inability, both of the President and Vice President, declaring what Officer shall then act as President, and such Officer shall act accordingly, until the Disability be removed, or a President be elected.

The President shall, at stated Times, receive for his Services, a Compensation, which shall neither be encreased nor diminished during the Period for which he shall have been elected, and he shall not receive within that Period any other Emolument from the United States, or any of them.

Before he enter on the Execution of his Office, he shall take the following Oath or Affirmation: "I do solemnly swear (or affirm) that I will faithfully execute the Office of President of the United States, and will to the best of my Ability, preserve, protect and defend the Constitution of the United States."

The Executive Power

Article II, Section 1, establishes the existence of an independent executive authority residing in the office of the Presidency, and it also establishes the link between presidential power and public opinion. It begins: "The executive power shall be vested in a President. . . ." Gouverneur Morris revised the vesting clauses in order to distinguish executive and legislative power. Article I begins with the phrase "All legislative Powers herein granted." Under Morris's formulation, the legislative powers of the government are limited to those specifically granted by the Constitution, but the executive power is subject to no such limitation.[7]

There are two possible reasons for such a distinction. First, it might be argued that the executive power is by nature limited. To "execute" means to carry out the laws. In this view, the power of the executive is expressly derived from the laws and therefore inherently subject to the limits of law. But there is another possible interpretation: The executive power is not limited, because by its very nature it cannot be subject to specific limitations. The executive is to execute the laws in particular circumstances, and the diversity of those circumstances is potentially unlimited. The reason

---

7. For an account of the importance of Morris's contribution to the creation of the Presidency, see Donald L. Robinson, "Gouverneur Morris and the Origin of the American Presidency," *Presidential Studies Quarterly* 17 (Spring 1987), 319–28.

for establishing an independent executive in the first place was to have a branch of government capable of exercising the discretion necessary for effective execution of the laws. Morris probably wanted to state the President's powers in the broadest possible terms, but there is an ambiguity in the language, an ambiguity that can be clarified only by an examination of the constitutional context of the vesting clause.[8]

This question of executive independence and discretion arose immediately at the Convention in the course of the debate over the number of executives. On June 1 Roger Sherman argued against a unitary executive on the grounds that the executive was a mere creature of the legislature. The number of executives, Sherman contended, should therefore be subject to the will of the legislature.[9] This argument, however, was never accepted by the Convention. Even Edmund Randolph, who called the unitary executive the "foetus of monarchy," said that the executive should be independent of the legislature.[10] By June 4 the Convention had decisively rejected the plural executive, and the first serious proposal based on the principle of executive dependence on the legislature died quite early at the Convention.[11]

Presidential Selection

The longest part of Article II, Section 1, is devoted to the provisions for the election of the President. Those provisions have been the subject of a great deal of misunderstanding and deserve a detailed examination.

8. Although such commentators as Raoul Berger have contended that the vesting clause should be understood very narrowly (Berger, *Executive Privilege*, 52), Charles Thach argued that Morris created the open-ended vesting clause "with full realization of its possibilities." Thach continued: "At any rate, whether intentional or not, it admitted an interpretation of executive power which would give the President a field of action much wider than that outlined by the enumerated powers" (Charles Thach, *The Creation of the Presidency, 1775–1789* [Baltimore: Johns Hopkins University Press, 1969], 139). Richard Pious states the issue well, explaining, "The phrase 'The Executive Power' was a general term, sufficiently ambiguous so that no one could say precisely what it meant. It was possible that the words referred to more than the enumerated powers that followed, and might confer a set of unspecified powers." What is unambiguous, according to Pious, is that the vesting clause "made it clear that the powers of the office . . . were derived from the Constitution, not derived from or limited by the legislative powers granted Congress in Article I. See Richard Pious, *The American Presidency* (New York: Basic Books, 1979), 29.

9. Farrand, ed., *Records*, 1:65.

10. Ibid., 66. Randolph opposed the unitary executive but nonetheless concluded that the executive ought to be independent of the legislature.

11. The other extensive debate with major implications for executive independence dealt with the issue of reeligibility (see ibid., 2:33, 52, 102). This discussion also demonstrates that the majority sentiment at the Convention favored executive independence.

Although after June 4 virtually no one made an argument for executive dependence on the legislature, for most of the Convention legislative election was the accepted method of presidential selection. As early as June 1 James Wilson had called for direct popular election of the President. Wilson claimed that direct election was necessary for executive independence. A President chosen by the people would be independent of the legislature. His power would come from the people through the Constitution, not through the legislature. Only through popular election could the President be equal to the legislature.[12] On June 2 Wilson modified his proposal to call for election by electors chosen by the people, but this was not meant as a significant change and was never really considered as such by the leading members of the Convention.[13] The major alternatives were legislative election versus some form of popular election, either direct or indirect, and until the closing days of the Convention the majority of delegates remained committed to legislative election.

Why did it take so long for the idea of popular election to be accepted? In only a few cases did delegates support legislative election out of a belief in legislative supremacy. The reason had more to do with the political concerns of the small states than with the principles of popular election or legislative supremacy. As Charles Thach has explained, the balance of power on the question of the method of election, as on most other issues, rested with the small states. Their votes were determined in large part by the effect one method of election or the other would have on their relative power in the new government. Popular election was even briefly accepted on July 19, when the small states thought they might gain an advantage from it.[14] But when Madison pushed to eliminate any added weight for the small states in a popular election, the Convention retreated to legislative choice on July 24. When the Committee of Detail reported its article on the executive on August 6, legislative election was still the accepted method of selection.[15]

12. See ibid., 1:68–69.
13. Ibid., 80.
14. When a plan for an electoral college was introduced in which the states with a population of 200,000 would receive one elector, those with between 200,000 and 300,000 would get two electors, and those with more than 300,000 would get three electors, the small states were willing to relinquish their commitment to legislative election. Under such a plan they knew it would not be long, as their populations increased, before they each had three electors. However, when this fact became obvious the Convention immediately decided that this formula should be temporary and open to change as the population grew. At this point the small states retreated to legislative election. For a closer examination of this point and the broader argument that the resistance to popular election through an electoral college was based on the fears of the small states rather than a positive commitment to legislative supremacy, see Thach, *Creation of the Presidency*, esp. 101–3.
15. Farrand, ed., *Records*, 2:185.

Popular election was not finally accepted until the report of the Committee of Eleven on September 4.[16] Up until this time the issue of how the legislature would vote for the President had been avoided. The small states had hoped for a concurrent ballot, in which the House and the Senate would vote separately. Under such an arrangement the power of the small states in the Senate would give them a virtual veto power over the choice of the President. The large states preferred a joint ballot, where the votes of the Senate would be diluted when added to the votes of the larger House. When the issue came to the forefront of the debate, it was obvious that the Convention was moving in the direction of a joint ballot rather than a concurrent ballot. Faced with this prospect, the small states were open to a compromise. Gouverneur Morris and the Committee of Eleven were ready with such a compromise.

The Committee of Eleven recommended that the President be elected by electors, who were to be chosen in a manner to be determined by the state legislatures. Each state would receive a number of electors equal to their number of Senators and Representatives. Each elector would have two votes, one of which must go to a person not from the home state of the elector. The person receiving the most votes would become President if he received a number of votes equal to a majority of the number of electors. If no candidate had a number of votes equal to a majority of the number of electors, the Senate would select the President from among the top five candidates. The Senate would also make the selection in the event of a tie.[17] This provision was later modified so that the House of Representatives, voting by state, would choose the President if there was a tie or if no candidate received a number of votes equal to a majority of the number of electors.[18] This proposal became the constitutional method of presidential selection.

It has been argued that this final method of election was far from a victory for the proponents of direct popular election. Commentators such as John Roche have claimed that the presidential selection system did not represent a victory for any principled position, that it was, like the rest of the Constitution, a mere bundle of compromises.[19] Even some delegates at the Constitutional Convention saw it as a victory for legislative election, claiming that because no candidate was likely to receive a majority on the first ballot the election would usually devolve on the legislature. This argument was made by James Wilson, the foremost supporter of popular election. Wilson reluctantly gave his support to the plan only after the

16. Ibid.
17. Ibid., 497–98.
18. Ibid., 527.
19. John P. Roche, "The Founding Fathers: A Reform Caucus in Action," *American Political Science Review* 55 (December 1961), 799–816.

backup election was taken out of the hands of the Senate and given to the House of Representatives. He feared that if the backup election were left in the hands of the Senate the Convention would have created the basis for aristocracy. With the backup election in the hands of the House, Wilson saw the selection system as an acceptable if not desirable compromise.[20]

There is no doubt that many of the delegates supported the final method of election either reluctantly or because they thought the legislature would usually make the choice. But the most farsighted members of the Convention saw that the final selection system was an essentially popular one. Gouverneur Morris argued that because we would become more united as a nation after the adoption of the Constitution, men with national reputations would arise. It would be unlikely that the election would often be thrown into the House of Representatives. Moreover, it would take only a number of votes equal to a majority of the number of electors to elect a President. This would be only 25 percent of the votes cast, because each elector has two votes.[21] Although the dynamics of the system were changed by the creation of political parties and the adoption of the Twelfth Amendment, it remains true that the provisions for presidential election, as established by the Constitutional Convention, encouraged popular election rather than legislative election of the President.

It is also commonly assumed that the use of electors was a product of the Framers' distrust of popular opinion. In support of this claim we are often treated to quotations from delegates to the Convention such as George Mason, who said: "It would be as unnatural to refer the choice of a proper character for chief Magistrate to the people, as it would be to refer a trial of colours to a blind man."[22] There is, however, a major problem with using such statements to show the antidemocratic character of the electoral college. The delegates who expressed the greatest distrust of popular choice were delegates who eventually opposed the Constitution, such as George Mason or Elbridge Gerry, or those who favored election by the legislature, such as Charles Pinkney, Roger Sherman, or George Mason.[23]

The most avid supporters of the electoral college were those who were

20. Farrand, ed., *Records,* 2:521.

21. Ibid., 511.

22. Ibid., 29.

23. See ibid., 1:80, 2:114, for Gerry's suspicions of popular election, and 1:175 for his proposal for election by the executives of the states; see 2:29 for Sherman's criticisms of the people as ill-informed and his preference for legislative election; see 2:30 for Pinkney's argument that the people would be led by a few "active and designing men" and his support for legislative election; and see 2:31 for Mason's comment on the blindness of the people in choosing a President and his support for legislative election.

seeking the most popular method of election likely to be accepted by the Convention and workable in practice.[24] The electoral college allowed for a compromise between small states and large states. The small states could receive added weight in the electoral college based on their equal representation in the Senate. The same principle that had been used to settle the dispute between the small states and the large states in regard to legislative apportionment could be applied to presidential selection.

Moreover, the electoral college compromise avoided a potential conflict between the North and the South. As Madison, an ardent supporter of popular election and the electoral college, explained, the different voting requirements and election laws in the different states made a simple direct election difficult. To attempt to reconcile those differences at the Constitutional Convention would have proved fruitless and perhaps placed the success of the entire Convention in jeopardy.[25] For example, it would have been impossible to adopt the principle of the three-fifths compromise in a direct popular election for the President. Without such a compromise, the slave states would either have had to give up any claim to electoral strength based on their slave populations or have had to grant slaves the right to vote. Either possibility might have been sufficient to cause the Southern states to withhold support from the Constitution.[26] Creation of the electoral college overcame some of those practical difficulties, while grounding the President's election in popular opinion.

But what of Alexander Hamilton's argument in the *Federalist*? There Hamilton claimed that the electoral college would refine popular opinion, would prevent the worst aspects of popular opinion from operating in the selection of the President.[27] Some delegates probably supported the electoral college because they saw it as a check on popular opinion. But it is interesting to note that Hamilton's argument in the *Federalist* for the refining effect of the electoral college was not made at the Constitutional Convention. Instead, Gouverneur Morris argued that the extent of the nation would serve to refine popular choice. Morris contended that al-

24. Clearly the delegates who spoke most in favor of democratic election of the President, such as Wilson, Madison, and Gouverneur Morris, were also the strongest supporters of the electoral college (Thach, *Creation of the Presidency*, 100).

25. Farrand, ed., *Records*, 1:111.

26. Donald L. Robinson provides a solid discussion of the importance of the slavery issue in regard to presidential selection. He notes that on July 17 Hugh Williamson of North Carolina complained that the slave states would not have as much power in a direct popular election and that Madison made a similar point on July 19. See Donald L. Robinson, *"To the Best of My Ability": The Presidency and the Constitution* (New York: W. W. Norton & Co., 1987), 82–83.

27. Hamilton explains the refining character of the electoral college in *Federalist* No. 68 (Alexander Hamilton, James Madison, and John Jay, *The Federalist*, ed. Jacob E. Cooke [Cleveland: Meridian Books, 1961], 458).

though persons of dubious character and ability might be elevated to office in a single district or state, they would be unlikely to be elected by the nation as a whole. Only worthy candidates would have a chance of gaining election from so large a constituency.[28] For Morris it was the size of the nation, and not the judgment of the electors, that would screen unworthy candidates. Hamilton borrows Morris's language for use in the *Federalist*, but he substantially alters Morris's argument.

Hamilton's argument is not refuted by the mere existence of Morris's claim. It is possible that Morris or other members of the Constitutional Convention misunderstood the principles animating the Constitution. It is also possible that Hamilton may have recognized more fully than the delegates at the Convention the need for a screening process in the selection of the President. But Hamilton's argument proved inadequate in explaining the operation of the system established by the Constitution. In practice, the system was more essentially democratic than even Hamilton's argument implied. The electors never exercised independent judgment to refine popular opinion. Historically they served only as a means of calculating popular opinion. Hamilton may have been right about the need for a screening process, but that process was to be developed outside of the Constitution by political parties.[29] It is paradoxical that Gouverneur Morris, a man frequently identified as one of the more aristocratic of the delegates at the Convention, best explained the popular character of the selection system established by the Constitution. He recognized and spoke with great approval of the democratic foundation of the constitutional Presidency. In a major speech on executive power on July 19, Morris contended that the people at large would be the best judge of presidential performance. He went on to argue: "The Executive magistrate should be the guardian of the people, even of the lower classes, against legislative tyranny."[30] In this view, the President's power was derived from and in the service of popular opinion. The President owed his legitimacy and independence to popular election, and because of his unique claim to represent national public opinion he would serve as a valuable counterweight to the legislature.[31]

28. Farrand, ed., *Records*, 2:54.

29. Even Hamilton spoke of the electoral college as a species of popular election. Defending reeligibility, Hamilton argued that the people would be able to judge whether or not an incumbent had done a good job. He saw elections as a kind of retrospective popular judgment. See Cooke, ed., *The Federalist*, 487–88.

30. Farrand, ed., *Records*, 2:52.

31. Even anti-Federalist critics of the Constitution recognized the popular character of the Presidency. An "Old Whig" suggested that he would prefer a hereditary monarch to the popularly elected President of the Constitution. He complained that under the constitutional provisions "we shall be embroiled in contention about the choice of the man," and

Thus the idea of a powerful popular executive did not arise with the Progressives. On this point, each of the three contemporary schools of presidential scholarship are defective. Both the extraconstitutional Presidency school and the constitutional restraint school fail to appreciate the Founders' desire for a strong Presidency, while the strong constitutional Presidency school neglects the popular sources of strength on which the Founders clearly wished to draw.

Institutional Incentives and Restraints

The remaining provisions of Section 1 provide institutional incentives that will increase the likelihood that a competent and independent President will be selected. The requirements for office illustrate the character of institutional incentives. For example, there is no magic age or number of years of residence, but on balance the requirements encourage a certain amount of maturity, knowledge of the people, attachment to the nation, and an ability to serve as a symbol of the nation.

The provisions for Vice-President suggest the possibility of removal in a republican government and the need for an orderly means of transition. They also show that—unlike the Congress, which will go out of session or which can survive without individual members—the nation always needs to have a President.

The compensation provisions are meant to encourage independence. A speech delivered by Benjamin Franklin points to the issue in a strange way. Franklin argued that the President should not be paid because a salary would attract the wrong kind of person to the office.[32] Franklin believed that the President should be someone who had little concern for selfish material gain. He might well have envisioned people like the Roosevelts, whose freedom from financial worries allowed a single-minded dedication to public service. No one took Franklin's argument seriously. This is probably a tribute to the dominance of democratic as opposed to aristocratic sentiments at the Convention. But the delegates wanted to avoid a conflict between public interest and private gain and avoid the appearance of such conflict. That is why the President's salary cannot be increased or diminished during the term of office.

The oath of office first points to the fact that the powers are exercised

---

the election "will be a scene of horror and confusion." ("An Old Whig, No. 5," in *The Complete Anti-Federalist*, ed. Herbert J. Storing [Chicago: University of Chicago Press, 1981], vol. 3, sec. 3, par. 31).

32. Farrand, ed., *Records*, 1:81.

through the constitutional office of the Presidency. The President is not sworn to follow the popular mandate of the people, but to uphold the office of the Presidency. Political power is ultimately derived from the people, but it is derived from the people through the Constitution. The oath also suggests a peculiar relationship between the President and the Constitution. The President is, "to the best of [his] ability, [to] preserve, protect and defend the Constitution." No other constitutional officer is given such a broad charge, nor is any other oath specifically provided in the Constitution. The oath presents at best an ambiguous claim to power, but it does suggest the personal character of the office.[33]

ARTICLE II, SECTION 2

The President shall be Commander in Chief of the Army and Navy of the United States, and of the Militia of the several States, when called into the actual Service of the United States; he may require the Opinion, in writing, of the principal Officer in each of the executive Departments, upon any Subject relating to the Duties of their respective Offices, and he shall have Power to grant Reprieves and Pardons for Offenses against the United States, except in cases of Impeachment.

He shall have Power, by and with the Advice and Consent of the Senate, to make Treaties, provided two thirds of the Senators present concur; and he shall nominate, and by and with the Advice and Consent of the Senate, shall appoint Ambassadors, other public Ministers and Consuls, Judges of the supreme Court, and all other Officers of the United States, whose Appointments are not herein otherwise provided for, and which shall be established by Law; but Congress may by Law vest the Appointment of such inferior Officers, as they think proper, in the President alone, in the Courts of Law, or in the Heads of Departments.

The President shall have Power to fill up all Vacancies that may happen during the Recess of the Senate, by granting Commissions which shall expire at the End of their next Session.

The provisions of Section 2 provide the President with a list of essentially executive powers. These powers grow out of a strain of thought ex-

33. There was little discussion of the oath at the Constitutional Convention. The provision calling for the President to "preserve, protect and defend the Constitution" was added

pressed most radically but also most clearly by Hamilton in his June 18 speech.[34] Whereas James Wilson argued that the source of executive independence and strength would be popular election, Hamilton contended that executive independence would require institutionally protected powers that would insulate the President from immediate popular opinion. Although Hamilton's proposals were seen as extremely antidemocratic, even by Hamilton's contemporaries, they highlighted a concern shared by many of the delegates at the Convention: How can institutional supports be provided for the stability and energy necessary to stand against the occasional follies of short-term public opinion?

Hamilton's June 18 speech called for life tenure for the executive, an absolute veto, the power to direct war once authorized by Congress, the unqualified power to appoint the secretaries of foreign affairs, war, and finance, the power to appoint with the approval of the Senate all other secretaries, the power to make treaties with the approval of the Senate, and the power to pardon all offenses except treason.

Hamilton's proposed system of government would be grounded in consent, but the emphasis of the system would be on providing stability and adequate power for the government. For example, life tenure would create an office that would not be subject to effects of short-term popular opinion. The proposal for life tenure follows in the tradition of Locke and Montesquieu, and it was defended by James Madison as being at least worthy of consideration.[35] It was even accepted briefly by Morris, but it was never accepted by the Convention as a whole because it denied an ongoing role for consent in the operation of the executive.[36] The Founders went further than Hobbes and Locke in providing a role for consent in the operation of government. Theirs would be a popular executive subject to reelection every four years.

The other provisions of Hamilton's plan are not as radical as they initially appear to be. The President was in fact made commander-in-chief of the armed forces, and although he was not given an absolute veto over legislation, he was given a qualified veto. The appointment power was given to the President, being modified from Hamilton's proposal only to the extent of requiring Senate approval for all appointments. The treaty-making power was placed in the hands of the President, with the qualifi-

---

at the suggestion of Mason and Madison on August 27, but no explanation for the change was presented (ibid., 2:427).

34. Ibid., 1:282–93, 304–11.

35. John Locke, *Two Treatises of Government,* with intro. and notes by Peter Laslett (New York: New American Library, 1965), 476; Montesquieu, *The Spirit of the Laws,* trans. Thomas Nugent (New York: Hafner Press, 1949), 158; Farrand, ed., *Records,* 2:34.

36. Farrand, ed., *Records,* 2:33.

cation of consent by the Senate, just as Hamilton proposed. Finally, the constitutional pardoning power went beyond Hamilton's proposal, allowing the President to pardon even the offense of treason.

Although prophetic, most of these proposals were not accepted until late in the Convention, and then with little discussion. It can only be concluded that the Convention was prepared for acceptance by the general arguments being made for an independent executive, and it is also probably true, as some cynical commentators have pointed out, that a number of delegates were ready to accept anything in order to go home.

Commander-in-Chief

The only essentially executive power granted to the President early in the Convention was the power of commander-in-chief. To understand this power, we must look to its constitutional context and to the competing congressional claims to the constitutional right to exercise the war power found in Article I.

ARTICLE I, SECTION 8

The Congress shall have the Power To lay and collect Taxes, Duties, Imposts and Excises, to pay the Debts and provide for the common Defence and general Welfare of the United States; but all Duties, Imposts and Excises shall be uniform throughout the United States;

To define and punish Piracies and Felonies committed on the high seas, and Offenses against the Law of Nations:

To declare War, grant Letters of Marque and Reprisal, and make Rules concerning Captures on Land and Water;

To raise and support Armies; but no Appropriation of Money to that Use shall be for a longer Term than two Years;

To provide and maintain a Navy;

To make Rules for the Government and Regulation of the land and naval Forces;

To provide for calling forth the Militia to execute the Laws of the Union, suppress Insurrections and repel Invasions:

To provide for organizing, arming, and disciplining, the Militia, and for governing such Part of them as may be employed in the Service of the United States, reserving to the States respectively, the

Appointment of the Officers, and the Authority of training the Militia according to the discipline prescribed by Congress.

The powers of Congress in relation to the conduct of war are clearly extensive. The Congress declares war, it raises and supports the army and the navy, and it provides rules for the organization and conduct of the armed forces. It is even implied in the provisions regarding letters of marque and reprisal and captures on land and water that the Congress plays a substantial role in the conduct of military actions short of war. Furthermore, it is clear that the Constitution intends to keep the military on a relatively short leash by limiting appropriations for the military to two years. In the face of this array of powers, the power of commander-in-chief might appear to be a very limited one.[37]

Yet we must remember that the number of powers may not be the best means of understanding the amount or extent of power. How much discretion does the President have, and how much control can Congress exercise? These questions are not settled by the Constitution, which does not attempt to draw a precise legal boundary between congressional and presidential war powers. Instead, the Constitution grants different powers to different institutions. Policy-making will result from the interplay of these complex powers. Hamilton best expressed the spirit of the Constitution in his "Pacificus Letters." The different branches of government, he claimed, possess concurrent powers. Each branch of the government has a claim to an independent source of authority in the area of war powers.[38] The fact that the authority of the branches may overlap does not undermine the existence of these independent powers. What it does do is force each branch to recognize the legitimacy of the other's actions when it itself prepares to act. The exercise of authority by one branch of government inevitably shapes the context in which the other branch must act.

The executive, for example, can never escape the requirements of congressional funding when in pursuit of any medium or long-range military policy. This is as true today as it was immediately following the adoption of the Constitution. But congressional action may also substantially increase the importance of the executive's authority. Once the armed forces are called into service, the President exercises a certain amount of discretion over their use. By providing for what are in practice a standing army

37. The argument that the legislature is supreme with regard to the war power is presented clearly and succinctly by David Gray Adler, "The President's War-Making Power," in *Inventing the American Presidency*, ed. Thomas E. Cronin (Lawrence: University Press of Kansas, 1989), 119–53. See also Schlesinger, *The Imperial Presidency*.

38. Alexander Hamilton, "The First Letter of Pacificus" (June 29, 1793), in *The Power of the Presidency*, ed. Robert S. Hirschfield (New York: Atherton, 1968), 57.

and a standing navy, Congress elevates the importance of the commander-in-chief power. The President does not have to wait for Congress to create an army or navy; they are already available to the President as a tool of policy. In the absence of specific prohibitions, the President can, for example, position the armed forces in such a way as to shape the policy options of the United States and to restrict the ability of Congress to redefine those options.

The relationship between congressional and executive war powers is much the same as the relationship between executive and legislative power more broadly considered. The powers of Congress are stated more explicitly. They are largely legal powers: Congress appropriates funds, makes rules concerning the conduct of the armed forces, and formally declares war. In no case, however, does it act. A declaration of war creates the legal condition of war but does not make war.[39]

Initially Congress was given the power to make war by the Constitutional Convention, but Madison and Gerry suggested substituting the power to declare war for the power to make war. They claimed that such a substitution would leave "to the executive the power to repel sudden attacks."[40] The proposal was adopted with virtually no discussion. It is impossible to determine the extent of the President's power to repel attacks from the comments made at the Convention, but the distinction James Madison and Elbridge Gerry made is indicative of the difference between congressional and executive power.[41] No one disputed the desir-

39. Donald Robinson makes a somewhat different distinction, claiming that the provisions of the Constitution give "Congress the power of supply and the President the power of command" (Robinson, *To the Best of My Ability*," 121). My interpretation and Robinson's both point to a Congress that provides the conditions for action and a President who acts.

40. Farrand, ed., *Records,* 2:318.

41. Adler claims that this distinction should be understood narrowly. It was created only to allow the President to respond to sudden attacks. He argues that commander-in-chief is a subordinate military position that must be under the control of a political superior—Congress. On the other hand, he contends that the term "declare" should be understood very broadly as a synonym for commence or initiate. He concludes, therefore, that the war-making power resides in Congress, with only one narrow exception—the power to repel sudden attacks. But this conclusion does not necessarily follow from his argument. One could grant him the proposition that only Congress can initiate offensive hostilities, but still find a broad scope for defensive actions. Indeed, I can think of no instance in which a President has used military force when he has not had at least some plausible claim to be defending the United States, its possessions, citizens, armed forces, or treaty obligations. The real issue is who directs the troops once they are called into the service of the United States. The answer is the commander-in-chief. The purpose of the commander-in-chief power is not to make the President subservient to Congress, as Adler suggests, but to make the military subservient to a popular constitutional officer—the President. Ultimately Adler rejects this notion because he is committed to the theory of legislative supremacy. He quotes approv-

ability of allowing the executive to respond to attack. When action is most necessary, it is the executive that is best suited to action. The key to the source of the executive's authority in relation to the war power lies in its ability to perform necessary acts. The reason for the creation of an independent executive is that Congress cannot act effectively. The reason the President is not a king or a tyrant is that he must act within the context of the Constitution.

It is in the case of war powers that the tension between law and action and between the legislature and the executive can be seen in its broadest outlines. The genius of the Constitution is that it attempts to comprehend both elements of that tension. The Constitution creates different types of war powers that will act in different ways to influence the exercise of the war power in any given circumstance. It provides guidelines for the management of that tension, but it does not and should not settle the precise boundaries of the war powers.

The "Opinions in Writing" Clause

The most puzzling provision of Article II, Section 2, is the "opinion in writing" clause, which states: "[The President] may require the Opinion, in writing, of the principal Officer in each of the executive Departments, upon any Subject relating to the Duties of their respective Offices...." The origin of this clause can be traced to the idea of an executive council proposed by Morris as a means of strengthening the executive. Morris wanted to provide constitutionally for the major offices of the executive department. By creating the offices in the Constitution, Morris wanted to ensure that the development of the executive branch would not be at the mercy of Congress.[42] The idea of the Council was dropped, however, because it was seen as a threat to executive independence. Some members of the Convention thought that such a council might compete with the President over the control of the administration of government. The "opinion in writing" clause is the only remnant of the original proposal.

This remnant, however, may be more important than it initially appears to be. First, the clause suggests a basis for executive privilege, because Congress is nowhere given the power to require opinions in writing of

---

ingly Roger Sherman's comment that the executive is "nothing more than an institution for carrying out the will of the legislature," but he fails to note that Sherman's argument was decisively rejected by the Convention. Adler's narrow reading of the President's war powers stands only if we accept a theory of the separation of powers rejected by the Convention.

42. Farrand, ed., *Records*, 2:342–44.

department heads or other administrative officers. More important, however, is that it is one of the few provisions that establishes a superior-subordinate relationship between the President and the bureaucracy. It points to a possible difference in the relationship between Congress and administrators and between the President and administrators.[43] Administrators serve Congress by serving the law, to the extent that the law provides specific guidance for their actions. However, to the extent that the execution of the law requires discretion, the exercise of that discretion is under the control of the President. He oversees the *opinions* that guide the exercise of administrative discretion.

Less may have been more in this case. The oversight of discretion is clearly more important to the development of an independent executive power than a constitutional list of cabinet offices. It may also be less restrictive of executive growth and development. What remains of Morris's proposal is not a pathetic remnant of an executive council but the essential element of the President's claim to executive independence.

The Pardoning Power

The pardoning power presents a fitting counterpoint to the commander-in-chief power. As commander-in-chief the President has discretion over the use of the total force of the United States. The pardoning power gives him the discretion to withhold the exercise of power over individual citizens. There are practical reasons for assigning the power to the President. Because mistakes will be made or extenuating circumstances will exist, a pardoning power is necessary. Congress is too numerous to exercise such a power, and the courts will have already rendered their judgment. It is also positively appropriate for the President to exercise this discretionary power, because it is he who will ultimately execute the sentence. The pardoning power may be the least subject to limits of any power in the Constitution. It is not surprising that in a limited government the least restricted power is the power to restrict the exercise of power. It is also not surprising that in modern liberal government this least restricted power would be given to the President.[44]

43. Thach, *Creation of the Presidency,* 123, makes a similar argument.

44. As an advocate of a strict legal definition of executive power, Adler is troubled by the open-endedness of the pardoning power and suggests that the Constitution was in error in not placing some check on the pardoning power. He even supports a constitutional amendment proposed by Walter Mondale that would make the pardoning power subject to override by a two-thirds vote of each house. See David Gray Adler, "The President's Pardon Power," in *Inventing the American Presidency,* 209–35. In one sense Adler is correct. If you believe that we have strictly a government of laws, then there is no room for a pardoning power. But

Qualified Powers

The second paragraph of Article II, Section 2, contains the powers that are exercised by the President but that require the advice and consent of the Senate. The position of these powers in the Constitution is an important indicator of their character. Just as the veto is described in Article I and not in Article II, because the veto is essentially legislative, the Senate's check on the President in regard to treaty-making and appointments is described in Article II rather than in Article I. Senate participation is in the character of a veto. The Senate cannot appoint or negotiate a treaty; it can only react to the President's action.

Treaty-making was originally assigned to the legislature, and even Hamilton conceded that treaty-making "partake[s] more of the legislative than of the executive character, though it does not seem strictly to fall within the definition of either of them."[45] Eventually, however, the President was given the power to make treaties with the concurrence of two-thirds of the Senate. Although Hamilton argued that treaties have the force of law, he also explained that treaties are not the same as law. Treaties are contracts negotiated between sovereigns. That is one reason treaties are not drafted or approved by normal legislative procedures.

The positive argument for giving the power to the President is that one person is better suited to negotiate treaties than an assembly or a committee. One person possesses the qualities of decision, secrecy, and dispatch that are necessary in treaty negotiations.[46] Moreover, although the President does not have the sovereign power of a king, he is clearly the representative of the sovereign power of the nation in treaty negotiations; he is not the representative of Congress. As Hamilton argued, if the President were understood to be a mere "ministerial servant of the Senate,"

> [he] could not be expected to enjoy the confidence and respect of foreign powers in the same degree as the constitutional representative of the nation; and of course would not be able to act with an equal degree of weight or efficacy.[47]

It is the President who will present the bargaining position of the United States to other nations; it is the President who will respond to the

---

the existence of an unqualified pardoning power in the Constitution suggests that the Founders, unlike Adler, believed there were limits to the rule of law. From the beginning, they understood that the Constitution must make room for discretion.

45. Cooke, ed., *The Federalist*, 504.

46. Ibid., 434–35.

47. Ibid., 506.

proposals of other nations; and it is the President who will be responsible for drafting a treaty. The initiative for treaty negotiations clearly rests with the President. The Senate can reject a treaty, and the Congress as a whole may in effect overturn a treaty by failing to pass legislation necessary for implementation. Thus any President would be foolish to disregard the wishes of the legislature, but it would also be foolish to deny the primacy of the President's role in the treaty-making process. The institutional arrangements established by Article II make the President in theory and in practice the focal point of the treaty-making process.

It is even more clear that the appointment power is essentially executive.[48] According to arguments made at the Convention and in the *Federalist,* presidential appointment promotes administrative responsibility.[49] It was recognized that administrators would exercise discretion and that there would be a need for a political check on the exercise of such discretion. It would be impossible for administrators to be responsible to a body as numerous as the legislature. The President, as one individual, is better suited to directing the actions of the administration and is more readily held accountable. The Senate's role in appointment is clearly a check, but only a check. The President cannot be forced to appoint someone of whom he disapproves. The Senate can only question the President's choice. Even in regard to inferior offices, the Congress cannot directly appoint. The power may be given to the President alone, to department heads, or to the courts. Administrative discretion need not always be under the direct control of the President, but it is never under the control of Congress.

The Power to Act

Recess appointments further enhance the President's power over administration. They are in part a response to a practical problem—government needs to act when Congress is not in session. They also serve to overcome the threat of inaction if the President and Congress reach a stalemate over an appointment. If the Senate refuses to approve a presidential nominee, the President would be able to appoint someone of his choosing when Congress is out of session. Thus a stalemate would be prevented; the President could always act through his chosen appointee.

The key to all the powers outlined in Section 2 is that they provide

48. In defending the Senate's role in impeachment, Hamilton argues that its role in the appointment process is a limited one and that the appointment power is essentially executive. See ibid., 449–50.

49. Ibid., 517–18.

pools of discretionary authority under the control of the President. The pools are circumscribed by the acts of the other branches, but the discretionary acts of the President also affect the discretionary authority of the other branches. When he directs the movement of troops, when he uses discretion in the implementation of a law, when he negotiates treaties, and when he nominates appointees, the President acts in a way that limits the discretion of his coordinate branches.

ARTICLE II, SECTION 3

> He shall from time to time give to the Congress Information of the State of the Union, and recommend to their consideration such Measures as he shall judge necessary and expedient; he may, on extraordinary Occasions, convene both Houses, or either of them, and in Case of Disagreement between them, with Respect to the Time of Adjournment, he may adjourn them to such Time as he shall think proper; he shall receive Ambassadors and other public Ministers; he shall take Care that the Laws be faithfully executed, and shall Commission all the Officers of the United States.

The provisions of Section 3 are not really powers at all; they are functions performed by the President because he represents the nation as a whole.[50] He is the best representative of the unified sovereign power of government. He does not possess this unified authority, but in representing it he wields a great deal of influence. These provisions were assigned to the President relatively early in the Constitutional Convention—most were suggested in the report of the Committee of Detail.[51] They were

---

50. To the extent that these powers receive any systematic treatment in the literature on the Presidency, it is argued that they are indicative of the President's role as chief of state—not a bad way of understanding Section 3. As chief of state, the President exercises a popular symbolic leadership role. See, for example, the discussion of the chief of state in *Guide to the Presidency*, ed. Michael Nelson (Washington, D.C.: Congressional Quarterly Press, 1989), 573–98.

51. After a short paragraph on the election and term of office of the President, the Report of the Committee of Detail immediately turns to the provisions that will eventually be incorporated in Article II, Section 3, of the Constitution. The second paragraph devoted to the executive reads as follows: "He shall from Time to Time give information [to the Legislature] of the State of the (Nation to the Legislature) [Union]; he may recommend (Matters) [such measures as he shall judge necessary. & expedt.] to their Consideration, and (he) may convene them on extraordinary Occasions [& in Case of a disagreement between the 2 Houses with regard to the Time of Adj. he may adjourn them to such Time as he shall think proper].

more readily accepted than the provisions of Section 2, perhaps because they were less threatening. They were understood to convey no explicit power. It is appropriate that they were proposed in a report written largely by James Wilson. The provisions are suited to a popular President who would govern by virtue of influence as much as by authority. As the only representative of the nation as a whole, the President would be able to yield a great deal of influence in the government, but the extent of the influence would clearly vary with the extent of the popularity of a particular President.

The State of the Union Address is perhaps the best example of the character of these provisions. The President can pass no legislation, and he cannot even formally introduce legislation. The President, however, is expected to play an agenda-setting role. He alone is called on to summarize the state of the union and to make recommendations appropriate to it. He alone possesses, by virtue of his institutional base and national election, the perspective from which to perform such a function. It is stated as a requirement rather than an option, because Gouverneur Morris feared a President would be reluctant to make recommendations.[52] He feared that such recommendations might be seen as an encroachment on the legislative power. By requiring presidential action, Morris ensured that the President would play an agenda-setting role.[53]

The power to convene the legislature and to adjourn it if the two houses disagree on the time of adjournment reflected another practical concern. The President is there to convene the legislature if there is an emergency. If there is a disagreement over adjournment, it would need to be settled.

(He shall take care to the best of his Ability, that the Laws) [It shall be his duty to provide for the due & faithful exec—of the Laws] of the United States (be faithfully executed) [to the best of his ability]. He shall commission all the Officers of the United States and (shall) appoint Officers in all Cases) ([such of them whose appts.) them in all cases] not otherwise provided by this Constitution. He shall receive Ambassadors, and shall correspond with the (Governours and other) [Supreme] Executives (Officers) of the several States." (Farrand, ed., *Records*, 2:171).

Although there is a rather open-ended discussion of the appointment power, and the following paragraph goes on to mention the pardoning power and the commander-in-chief power, the focus of the report is clearly on the aspects of the Presidency that eventually will be found in Section 3. Those provisions appear first, and they dominate the entire discussion of the executive power.

52. Ibid., 405.

53. In regard to this provision, Thach notes: "Executive influence on legislative measures is very generally spoken of as a modern development, entirely unforeseen by the framers of the Constitution, . . . yet we see that the idea of executive preparation and report of plans of legislation was very much alive [at the Convention]" (Thach, *Creation of the Presidency*, 124).

This provision reminds one of Locke's executive, who could convene and adjourn the legislature at will.[54] It is different from Locke's recommendation in that the President cannot adjourn the legislature at will. The Founders were less willing than Locke to do away with the legislature. It is similar to Locke in that the executive is the one who calls attention to the need for legislative action, and the President could, at least in theory, dissolve the legislature if he could convince one house to go along with him. Although this is a potentially extraordinary power, it is not likely to be used. It is most important as an example of the President as the focal point of government. Not only can he call the attention of the assembled legislature to particular problems, he can also assemble the members of the legislature in order to speak to them.

The provision to receive ambassadors could also be seen as another necessary but not very important chore. Somebody has to do it, and it would be awkward and confusing to have Congress perform the function. The question is whether the provision conveys any discretion. Some say no; they claim it is only a matter of convenience.[55] There is, however, no practical way to force the President to receive an ambassador he chooses not to receive. Moreover, there is no alternative to presidential discretion if competing sets of ambassadors are sent. It is a logical extension of provisions that make the President the national representative in foreign affairs in every circumstance: war, treaty negotiation, and day-to-day relations with other nations. It may not provide specific powers to the President, but it obviously involves influence in that the President will present the position of the United States to other nations.

The "take care" clause has been used to legitimate broad exercises of discretionary authority, but its placement in Section 3 gives reason to question its conferral of extraordinary powers.[56] If it had appeared at the

54. Locke, *Two Treatises*, 416–17.

55. Adler argues that the recognition power was not meant to give the President any discretionary authority and quotes Hamilton and Madison on its limited scope. See David Gray Adler, "The President's Recognition Power: A Towering Structure" (Paper delivered at the 1986 American Political Science Convention, August 28–31, 1986). Adler is probably correct that Madison and Hamilton failed to see the potential importance of the recognition power, but what Adler fails to explain is where in the Constitution he finds a basis for congressional control of that power. Again he must rely on his assumption that the Constitution created a system of legislative supremacy, but there is nothing in the text of the Constitution to support the idea of legislative supremacy in regard to the recognition power.

56. Thomas Cronin notes that an expansive reading of the "take care"clause is often associated with a expansive reading of the "vesting" clause. Both provisions are used to suggest that the President has "power above and beyond the enumerated or specified powers." Cronin concludes that at the very least the "take care" clause makes "the President the nation's primary administrator and together with the appointment power, has paved the way for

beginning of Article II, as does the vesting clause, or in the list of essentially executive powers found in Section 2 of Article II, a case could be made for viewing it as a broad grant of discretionary authority. But coming as it does in the context of Section 3, it is safer to interpret it as an extension of the President's representative function. The President is in the best position to call attention to problems in the execution of the law. He can focus public and congressional attention on the problem. He is, of course, free to use the other explicit powers at his disposal to encourage better execution of the laws. He may even appeal to the open-ended character of the vesting clause. But to rely on the "take care" clause alone as a grant of power is inconsistent with the logic of Article II.

The commissioning of officers is largely a ceremonial function. The President as the representative of the nation conveys its honors. This function also helps to build his basis of public influence and support. The White House Christmas card list may be more important today than commissioning of officers, but the principle at work remains the same. The President conveys honors and by doing so enhances his public support. It should be added that the President can also use this function to highlight issues or problems.

The constitutional position of the Presidency and its national popular election provide the basis for the exercise of tremendous political influence by the President. The provisions of Section 3 of Article II provide the constitutional foundation for the exercise of such influence. Presidents can learn much about political influence from the Constitution. The Progressives and Neustadt were right about the importance of popular leadership and political persuasion, but they were wrong in ignoring the constitutional foundations for these characteristics of the Presidency.

THE VETO POWER (ARTICLE I, SECTION 7)

Every Bill which shall have passed the House of Representatives and the Senate, shall, before it become a Law, be presented to the

---

presidents to become the nation's central agent in the administrative, regulatory, welfare, and warfare domains" (Thomas E. Cronin, "The President's Executive Power," in *Inventing the American Presidency*, 189–90). What is noteworthy about Cronin's comments is that in both cases he links the claim of substantial power in the "take care" clause with other provisions of the Constitution. Implied powers are found by looking at the "take care" clause in association with the "vesting" clause, and the President's role as chief administrator is explained by a combination of the "take care" clause and the appointment power. This is significant because it suggests the weakness of the "take care" clause by itself. In the spirit of Section 3, the President has responsibility as the national officer charged with overseeing the execution of the laws, but he carries out that responsibility directly only through the use of other executive powers.

President of the United States; If he approves he shall sign it, but if not he shall return it, with his Objections, to that House in which it shall have originated, who shall enter the objections at large on their Journal, and proceed to reconsider it. If after such Reconsideration two thirds of that House shall agree to pass the Bill, it shall be sent together with the Objections, to the other House, by which it shall be likewise reconsidered, and if approved by two thirds of that House, it shall become a Law. But in all such cases the Votes of both Houses shall be determined by Yeas and Nays, and the names of the Persons voting for and against the Bill shall be entered on the Journal of each House respectively. If any Bill shall not be returned by the President within ten Days (Sundays excepted) after it shall have been presented to him, the Same shall be a Law, in like Manner as if he had signed it, unless the Congress by their Adjournment prevent its Return in which case it shall not be a Law.

The most glaring deficiency in our analysis of presidential power thus far is the lack of a discussion of the veto power. The reason the veto has not yet been addressed is that the veto is not found in Article II of the Constitution. It is not found in Article II because it is an essentially legislative power. It exists first as a means of self-defense for the executive. The President can use the veto to protect himself against encroachments on his power by the legislature. It is also a check on possible errors by the legislature.

The debate over the veto at the Constitutional Convention centered on two questions: who would exercise the veto and whether it would be a qualified or absolute veto. Madison and Wilson called for a council of revision consisting of the President and the members of the Supreme Court, which would have the power to veto legislation.[57] Although the council was supported by some as a check on the President, most saw it as a means of giving extra weight to the veto. Madison argued that the President would be better able to stand against the legislature if he had the added weight of the Court behind him. The council was rejected early in the Convention on the grounds that it might undercut executive responsibility and independence and might also conflict with judicial review.[58]

---

57. See Farrand, ed., *Records*, 1:138–39. Later in the Convention, Madison and Wilson again proposed a Council, expanding on their earlier arguments (ibid., 2:73–74).

58. For the argument that the judiciary should not be included in a Council of Revision because it will have its own independent check, see Gerry's speech (ibid., 1:97–98). For the view that a Council would undercut executive independence, see comments by Gerry and King in ibid., 139.

The idea of an executive council was resurrected later, but not as a council of revision.[59]

An absolute veto was supported by Hamilton and Wilson as necessary to provide the President with sufficient strength to stand against the legislature.[60] Such a veto was of course feared by those who were afraid of a strong Presidency, and even by most moderates. Madison, however, made the most interesting argument against it, claiming that the veto would not be used if it were absolute. The President would not want to appear despotic in exercising an absolute veto. He would be more likely to use the veto, according to Madison, if he could point to at least some support in the legislature for his actions, and Madison clearly wanted the veto to be a viable presidential power.[61] The argument for an absolute veto was never accepted as being consistent with republican principles, but the idea of a limited veto was never seriously questioned.

The veto is only indirectly an executive power because the President can participate in legislation only indirectly. He can only say no. Nonetheless, the veto may serve to enhance the influence or the agenda-setting role of the President growing out of Section 3 of Article II. The veto was designed to be primarily a defensive tool of the President, but it may also serve to encourage Congress to take his suggestions regarding legislation more seriously than it otherwise would. The ability to say what he would not accept constitutes no positive power to implement that which he finds to be desirable, but it does enhance his influence.

IMPEACHMENT AND REMOVAL FROM POWER (ARTICLE II, SECTION 4)

> The President, Vice President and all civil Officers of the United States, shall be removed from Office on Impeachment for, and Conviction of, Treason, Bribery, or other high Crimes and Misdemeanors.

Although the President has numerous sources of power, he is a republican constitutional officer, and that is why an impeachment process is necessary. The Founders rejected an appeal to heaven as method of removal,

59. The Council of Revision proposed by Madison was to strengthen the veto power, but the executive council proposed by Morris was not intended to participate in the President's veto power. It was instead an attempt by Morris to establish a cabinet for the President in the Constitution. Farrand, ed., *Records*, 2:342–44.

60. See Farrand, ed., *Records*, 1:98.

61. Ibid., 99–101.

just as they rejected life tenure and a nonpopular election. Gouverneur Morris, however, was concerned about impeachment—he thought it might make the President dependent on the impeaching body.[62] But eventually the Founders were persuaded that in a limited republican government an impeachment process was necessary in order to avoid the need for revolution.

In the *Federalist* No. 65, Hamilton claims that impeachment and removal were assigned to the legislature primarily because there was no suitable alternative.[63] It was not a sign of legislative supremacy. The legislature does not act as a legislative body. It is divided into a prosecuting chamber and a trial chamber. The trial is to be presided over by the Chief Justice of the Supreme Court, and the Senators were to act under special oath.[64] Historically it has not been used as an instrument of policy-making, with the possible exception of the period of Reconstruction. It does not imply legislative supremacy any more than the legislature's inability to act implies executive supremacy.

Each branch has the potential to thwart the will of the other. Congress could impeach and remove the President over a mere policy disagreement, but the members of the legislature would be likely to pay a steep price at the next election. The President could refuse to act to carry out the laws passed by the legislature. The legislature could object. It could begin impeachment proceedings and eventually remove a particular President, but it could never act on its own. Congress is utterly dependent on a President to carry out its laws. Each branch may be rendered impotent by the other, and only by an appeal to the people can such a deadlock be overcome. It is this institutional version of deterrence theory that discourages the capricious use of the impeachment provisions or of the executive's discretion in administration.

THE CONSTITUTIONAL CONTEXT OF EXECUTIVE POWER

The most important check on the executive is the political forces set in motion by the Constitution. This discussion has emphasized the claims

62. Ibid., 2:53, 64–65.

63. In *Federalist* No. 65 (*The Federalist*, 441–45) Hamilton explains why neither the Supreme Court nor a special independent body would have been appropriate to conduct a trial of impeachment.

64. On September 8, Gouverneur Morris noted: "There could be no danger that the Senate would say untruly on their oaths that the President was guilty of crimes" (Farrand, ed., *Records*, 2:551).

of executive power in order to demonstrate that there is an essential authoritative and independent executive power, but other constitutional powers do circumscribe executive power, sometimes directly and sometimes indirectly. This does not lead to constant conflict, because the Constitution creates presumptions in favor of different branches in different circumstances. Ultimately conflict would result if each branch pushed its claims to their logical conclusion. The genius of the Constitution is that this has never happened. The different types of power are defined clearly enough that each branch can find a sufficient outlet for the exercise of discretion, and each branch has the opportunity to gauge the extent to which the people will ultimately be willing to accept its exercise of authority as legitimate.

The popular executive is perhaps the greatest contribution of the American Constitution to the theory and practice of modern liberal government. It mutes the conflict between consent and effective government. Unlike Hobbes's sovereign or even Locke's executive, the President is elected and reelected by the people. Oddly enough, it may be precisely this fact that gives rise to legitimate fears of tyranny. The danger is not that the President would be a king, the danger is that he would be a demagogue. This danger is countered by the existence of the other branches, and also by the President's recognition of institutional sources of authority and by his need to maintain those sources. Every President eventually recognizes the need to act in opposition to public opinion, and on such occasions he must rely on institutional sources of authority.

The popular constitutional office created by Article II does much to explain the development of the American Presidency. Development has indeed occurred, but for the most part the development of the office can be understood as logical outgrowths of the constitutional Presidency. Many of the specific developments were not anticipated by the Founders, but that does not alter the fact that most developments can be traced to the forces set in motion by the structure of the Constitution in general and of Article II in particular. The Constitution is largely responsible for the character of the modern Presidency.

By better understanding the constitutional Presidency, we can better understand both the operation of the modern Presidency and the elements of the contemporary political practice that are at odds with the constitutional Presidency. These elements are not to be rejected out of some simpleminded reverence for the Founders. This is not a game of "the Founders said," where any reform not specifically mentioned by the Founders is to be rejected out-of-hand. What we must recognize is that reforms that are at odds with the animating principles of our system of government will almost inevitably prove to be dysfunctional. Growth or reform must be adapted to its institutional context. By looking to the different aspects of the modern Presidency in the next three chapters, we shall see more clearly how the constitutional Presidency has developed and how its operation can be rendered more consistent with the animating principles of the political system.

CHAPTER THREE

Setting Legislative Priorities:

Presidential Leadership and the Budget Process

In this chapter and the two that follow, we use three case studies to examine the specific elements of the myth of the modern Presidency. First, we look at the legislative and popular leadership roles of the Presidency in the case of the budget process. In Chapter 4 we investigate the President's control of the executive branch through a study of the controversies surrounding the removal power and the legislative veto. And in Chapter 5 we explore the use of unilateral authority in the context of the debate over the President's war powers.

Even scholars who take a narrow view of the President's constitutional powers will usually admit that the Constitution provides a substantial role for the President in the areas of foreign policy and administration. The two aspects of the modern Presidency that are most alien to traditional conceptions of the Constitution are legislative leadership and popular leadership.[1] Under the Constitution, it is argued, Congress is the primary representative of popular opinion and it is Congress that is responsible

---

1. See Christopher J. Bosso, "Legislative Leader" in *Guide to the Presidency,* ed. Michael Nelson (Washington, D.C.: Congressional Quarterly Press, 1989), 457; Fred I. Greenstein, "Change and Continuity in the Modern Presidency," in *The New American Political System,* ed. Anthony King (Washington, D.C.: American Enterprise Institute, 1978), 45–46.

for establishing government policy by enacting laws. According to the myth of the modern Presidency, however, beginning with Franklin Roosevelt Presidents have assumed the roles of preeminent national popular leader and chief legislator. In so doing, modern Presidents have usurped important functions performed by Congress during the nineteenth century, functions that had been assigned to Congress by the Constitution.

Nowhere is this argument made more often or more forcefully than in regard to the power of the purse. The Constitution may have given the President a limited power to wield the sword of government, but the power of the purse was given unambiguously to the legislature. The primacy of the issue of taxation in the Revolutionary War, and the historical association of parliamentary control over governmental finances with the liberty of Englishmen, reenforced the notion that the legislature should dominate in budgetary matters.

By the 1970s, however, Congress believed that its power over the purse was dwindling and that more and more the President was setting and controlling the budgetary agenda.[2] Congress formulated no budget of its own. It began its deliberation with a budget submitted by the President and relied on the estimates and on projections by executive branch officials. Congress considered the budget only in pieces and was never able to offer the nation its own coherent set of budgetary priorities.[3] The number and complexity of governmental activities meant that Congress often left substantial discretion to the President in the specific allocation of funds. Finally, Congress was faced with the threat of a veto if the President opposed its actions.

Increasingly, members of Congress believed that the President had turned the Constitution on its head. He had assumed control of the budget process in complete contradiction of the provisions of the Constitution and the fundamental principles of democratic government. In the nineteenth century the President had for the most part recognized the constitutional limits of his office, and budgetary matters had remained under the control of the legislative branch.[4] But the twentieth century had

2. Allen Schick describes the period from 1966 to 1973 as the "seven-year budget war" both within Congress and between the President and Congress. See Allen Schick, *Congress and Money* (Washington, D.C.: Urban Institute, 1980), 17. See also Howard E. Schuman, *Politics and the Budget: The Struggle Between the President and Congress* (Englewood Cliffs, N.J.: Prentice Hall, 1992), 212–15.

3. For a discussion of the fragmentation of the congressional budget process, see the report of the House Rules Committee on the budget process in 1973: House Committee on Rules, *Budget and Impoundment Control Act of 1973: Report*, H. Rpt. 93-658, 93d Cong., 1st sess., 1973.

4. Donald F. Kettl provides a clear statement of this view, claiming that "for the first century of the American republic, Congress was the clear center of the budgetary process."

seen a constant subversion of the constitutional balance of authority in which the President had come to dominate in what was universally recognized to be the Congress's primary area of authority and responsibility. The budgetary reform movement that began in the mid-1970s was an attempt to reassert the primacy of Congress in budgetary matters and to reestablish the proper constitutional relationship between the Congress and the President on these issues.

A compelling case can be made that the President has become more involved in budgetary matters. The twentieth century has seen an unmistakable growth in the formal role of the President in the budget process. The establishment of the Bureau of the Budget in 1921 provided for the first comprehensive national budget and gave responsibility for that budget to the President. The expansion of the Bureau of the Budget and its increased control by the White House under Franklin Roosevelt further enhanced the President's role in the budgetary process. The increasing use of the budget as a priority-setting tool by Presidents from Truman to Nixon culminated in Nixon's transformation of the Bureau of the Budget to the Office of Management and Budget (OMB). By the 1980s, OMB directors, such as David Stockman and Richard Darman, were popularly recognized as among the most influential figures in Washington.

Today the President and the executive branch play a more active role in the budget process than nineteenth-century Presidents did. But that does not necessarily mean that the balance of power between the Congress and the President has shifted, or that the President has stepped outside of his constitutional office to assume control of Congress's most important constitutional prerogative. The change in the balance of power between the President and Congress from the nineteenth to the twentieth century is greatly exaggerated, and the contemporary role of the President in the budgetary process is a logical outgrowth of the constitutional office.

The myth of the modern Presidency ignores the fact that the Constitution provided the foundation for the President's role as popular leader by making the President the only person elected by the nation as a whole. Moreover, as the only national representative of the people, the President's voice would inevitably carry a great deal of weight in establishing the legislative agenda. The constitutional provision requiring the President to assess the state of the union and to recommend measures he deemed appropriate further enhanced the President's role in setting the legislative agenda.

See Donald F. Kettl, *Deficit Politics: Public Budgeting in Its Institutional and Historical Context* (New York: Macmillan Co., 1992), 124. See also Louis Fisher, *Presidential Spending Power* (Princeton: Princeton University Press, 1975).

Although the President was intended to play a leadership role in the entire field of domestic policy, it is in discussions of the budget that this role is most prominent. To the extent that we have a discussion of national priorities, that discussion takes place largely in the context of debate over the budget. And to the extent that Congress outlines a legislative agenda, that agenda arises through debate over the budget. As the only unified representative of the nation, the President is the most prominent single force in the articulation of national priorities and in the development of a comprehensive budget that reflects those priorities. Because the importance of the President's constitutional role has not been fully appreciated, most of the recent attempts at reform of the budget process have been misguided and ultimately unsuccessful.

The years following the passage of the 1974 Congressional Budget and Impoundment Control Act have represented a low point in the operation of the budget process. Only Reagan, in 1981 and 1982, briefly managed to use the process to any positive effect.[5] But the overall effect of the reform has been to support often meaningless budget resolutions, a frequent failure to pass appropriations bills, and an ever-growing budget deficit.[6] These problems led to additional reforms and proposals for reform, such as the line-item veto, the balanced-budget amendment, and the various versions of Gramm-Rudman.

None of these reforms or proposals for reform takes into account the different institutional characters of the different branches under the separation of powers. In the Congressional Budget and Impoundment Control Act, Congress ignored its role as the representative of the diverse interests of the nation and sought instead to imitate the President's unified national perspective. It ignored the institutional incentives created by relatively small single-member districts and relatively short terms of office, and the institutional difficulties in finding a single voice for 435 members of the House and 100 Senators. Presidential support for the line-item veto and a balanced-budget amendment is equally misguided. The line-item veto is based on legislative rather than executive powers, and the balanced-budget amendment would limit the discretion that is at the heart of executive

5. One might argue that the 1990 Budget Agreement developed in the Bush administration, and the first Clinton budget, represent successful uses of the budget process, but I contend that the mechanism of the congressional budget process was relatively unimportant in these two cases. Reagan used the budget resolution to force a definitive up or down vote on his budget proposals, but in the case of both Bush and Clinton more traditional bargaining between the President and Congress over specific appropriations and tax bills played a more important role than the initial vote on the congressional budget resolution.

6. Kettl, *Deficit Politics,* 129–32, makes a similar point, arguing that the period between 1974 and the present has been, with few exceptions, a period of budget stalemate.

power. Finally, Gramm-Rudman was based on the assumption that policy outcomes could be guaranteed by virtue of institutional reforms, an assumption that has consistently proved to be utopian. Institutional reforms like Gramm-Rudman are no substitute for legislative leadership and popular leadership, and in our constitutional system such leadership has always come from the President.

Although the constitutional balance of power tends to reassert itself, it is often thwarted and distorted by these misguided attempts at reform.[7] We need to recover a constitutional perspective. We need to remember that under the Constitution a unified perspective on policy, especially budget policy, most naturally arises in the executive branch. The initiation of policy and the representation of the national interest by the President have a clear constitutional foundation. Although the President cannot "make" policy in this area, he has considerable influence by virtue of his constitutional position.

Congress has a role, perhaps even the primary role, to play in domestic-policy-making, but policy is generally made in response to Presidential initiatives. Congress builds consensus, it weaves together the specific provisions of the policy, and it codifies the policy in law. But because it does not speak with a single voice it is not institutionally suited for sounding the call to action.

A REVISED HISTORY OF THE POLICY PROCESS

To say that Congress dominated the budget process in the nineteenth century is to miss one crucial point: To a large extent there was no budget process or budget policy in the nineteenth century. For most of the period, revenues were more than adequate to cover the limited expenses of the government. Budget surpluses allowed both the Congress and the President to avoid concern with overall budget policy.[8]

There was no unified budget, and to the extent that major initiatives

---

7. Nelson Polsby argues that, particularly since the passage of the 1974 Congressional Budget Act, the differences between the Presidential and the congressional budget processes have been significantly reduced. Congress now tries to take a more unified approach, and the President, like Congress, budgets incrementally, beginning with the numbers from the previous year's budget. See Nelson Polsby, *Congress and the Presidency*, 4th ed. (Englewood Cliffs, N.J.: Prentice Hall, 1986), 185–86. To some extent Polsby is correct, but my point is that this confusion of the two approaches has led each branch to misunderstand its own institutional capacities.

8. Even such scholars as Kettl, who speak of congressional dominance in the nineteenth century, admit that in the nineteenth century "there really was no budget" (see Kettl, *Deficit*

that changed the shape of budget policy were undertaken, they were, like today, largely presidential initiatives. It was the executive branch in the Washington administration that took the lead on the major budget policy issue of the day: the funding of the war debt. The victory of the administration's position on this issue was the most important budgetary decision of the early years of the nation.

The next major initiative undertaken by the federal government was the purchase of the Louisiana Territory by Jefferson. This was important not only because it represented a substantial commitment of government funds without prior congressional approval. Even more important is that by doubling the territory of the United States this presidential policy initiative created inevitable pressure for internal improvements in transportation and communication that would tie together a sprawling nation.

Up until the Civil War the issue of internal improvements remained one of the dominant issues regarding budget policy. Because of the pressures created by the Louisiana Purchase, Whig Congressmen provided some federal funding for internal improvements, but the level of funding remained relatively modest, in large part because of the Democratic majority created by Andrew Jackson. Jackson resisted expenditures for internal improvements because he believed in a limited national government and because he believed that by limiting government expenditures he could fulfill his campaign promise to pay off the national debt. Jackson did not stop the growth of the national government or the national budget, but he did slow it down, and he did establish a consensus that held sway for most of the period up to the Civil War.[9]

In the short run, the Civil War dramatically changed the budget of the federal government. The war effort under the direction of President Lincoln led to an enormous expansion in the federal budget. It also gave rise to one of the first major congressional reforms of the budget process: the creation of separate appropriations committees to oversee spending. But as in the case of the Louisiana Purchase, the more important effects were seen in the long run. After the Civil War, government support for internal

---

Politics, 125). Kettl quotes Leonard White, who claimed that there was "an extraordinary dispersion of responsibility for fiscal administration in numerous offices concerned with public finance, and a corresponding confusion of responsibility for fiscal policy in an incompetent and badly organized legislative body" (Leonard White, Introduction to the Study of Administration [New York: Macmillan Co., 1950], 250–51).

9. Everett Ladd describes the consensus reached between the Whigs and the Democrats of the period. He argues that there was no great contest between competing ideologies, but instead a basic agreement between the Whigs and the Democrats on the virtues of individualism and liberalism. See Everett Carl Ladd Jr., American Political Parties: Social Change and Political Response (New York: W. W. Norton & Co., 1970), 90–91.

improvements and industrial expansion increased to unprecedented levels. This rise in expenditures may not be traced directly to presidential initiatives in many cases, but the possibility for such a change was unquestionably the result of presidential initiative. As a congressional party, the Whigs had achieved only limited success in committing the resources of the federal government to building the infrastructure of a national economy. It was only after Lincoln, the former Whig, created a national majority for the Republican party that the Whig agenda would become the national agenda.[10]

The end of the nineteenth century was marked by the politics of spoils and special interests. The parochial and fragmented character of Congress was particularly well suited to such a period. It is not surprising that Congress appears to be the dominant branch in a period characterized by special-interest politics, because Congress was designed to represent specific local interests and to encourage compromise among those interests. But when attempts were made to transcend parochial interests, those attempts were generally initiated by the President. It was Rutherford B. Hayes, James Garfield, and Chester Arthur who sought to restrict the influence of local spoilsmen. And it was Grover Cleveland who became the most prolific presidential vetoer of the nineteenth century in response to what he perceived to be the unchecked growth in government expenditures.[11]

As we move into the twentieth century, we see many more presidential policy initiatives. But this change is explained by two factors: first, the tremendous change in society brought about by industrialization, urbanization, immigration, and a changing world order all created a host of new problems to be addressed by government;[12] second, in response to these problems the Progressives and others began to question the emphasis on limited government and to fashion a justification for more activist government.[13]

In this context, Presidents became more active in the policy arena, to deal with the greater demands placed on the government as a whole. As President, Theodore Roosevelt led the charge for more activist government. He and Woodrow Wilson placed a host of Progressive reforms on the national agenda. World War I provided a launching pad for an ever-growing and ever more complex federal government. As Greenstein and

10. Stephen B. Oates explains Lincoln's broad political agenda in "Republican in the White House," in *Abraham Lincoln and the American Political Tradition*, ed. John L. Thomas (Amherst: University of Massachusetts Press, 1986).

11. Fisher, *Presidential Spending Power*, 25.

12. Ladd, *American Political Parties*, 109–79.

13. See Herbert Croly, *The Promise of American Life* (Cambridge, Mass.: Harvard University Press, 1965).

many others have noted, Franklin Roosevelt, through the twin crises of depression and war, provided the impetus for the welfare state and military leadership of the United States that would continue to grow for the rest of the century.[14] The avalanche of issues placed on the national agenda permanently transformed the character of government and were largely the product of presidential leadership.

The growth in government activity led to an increased interest in the budget process. Theodore Roosevelt appointed the Keep Commission, which among other things recommended creation of an executive budget. Taft considered various proposals for budget reform, including one that not only would have allowed the President to submit a budget but also would have prevented Congress from appropriating any funds that would exceed the amounts recommended in the presidential budget.[15]

To a large extent, these proposals for reform grew out of increasing concern about budget deficits at the end of the nineteenth and the beginning of the twentieth century. As the deficits were reduced or eliminated during the Taft administration, the impetus for reform was lost. Only after World War I and its corresponding increase in the budget and in budget deficits did budget reform become a reality. The Bureau of the Budget was created in 1921, and for the first time there was a comprehensive presidential budget.[16] A consensus had emerged that a more active government in the twentieth century would require greater coordination of its budget. Although it took some time to reach this consensus, no one doubted that if greater unity and coordination were necessary they could come only from the executive branch.[17]

The creation of the Bureau of the Budget was an important milestone, but initially its functions were relatively limited. It was only to serve a centralized accounting function. Not until another major period of policy initiatives did the Bureau of the Budget become a tool for the direction of policy.[18] Franklin Roosevelt saw the possibility that the Bureau could be

---

14. Greenstein, "Change and Continuity," 47–53.

15. See William M. Goldsmith, ed., *The Growth of Presidential Power: A Documented History*, 3 vols. (New York: Chelsea House, 1974), 3:1471–78.

16. For a discussion of the origins of the Bureau of the Budget, see Howard E. Shuman, *Politics and the Budget: The Struggle Between the President and the Congress*, 3d ed. (Englewood Cliffs, N.J.: Prentice Hall, 1992), 25–35.

17. It is difficult to cite specific evidence for this contention because the evidence lies in what was not said. I have found no source that mentions a proposal to unify the budget that would have relied on Congress rather than the President. The assumption that greater control of the budget would come only from an executive budget would appear to have been unquestioned.

18. Stephen Hess, *Organizing the Presidency* (Washington, D.C.: The Brookings Institution, 1976), 39.

used as a way to set the priorities of the national government, a way to aid the President in controlling the policy agenda. To that end, he enlarged the office and moved it out of the Treasury Department, where it was originally housed, and into the offices of the White House. Since that move it has played an ever-growing role in setting the national policy agenda. Under Ronald Reagan, budget policy and the Office of Management and Budget moved out of the wings and came to play a dominant role in both foreign and domestic policy debates.

CONGRESSIONAL BUDGET REFORM

Even before Reagan, Congress had become concerned with its perceived loss of power in budgetary affairs, and in 1974 it passed the Congressional Budget and Impoundment Control Act. Support for the Budget Act came from a wide variety of sources. First and foremost were the opponents of the imperial Presidency of Richard Nixon. Members of Congress were particularly upset with Nixon's unilateral impoundment of funds appropriated by Congress, and the Act was seen as a way legally to restrict such impoundments. The impoundment provisions were probably the most successful part of the Act. But the opponents of the imperial Presidency believed that broader-scale budget reform was also necessary. The entire budget process as constituted left far too much power in the hands of the President. They wanted more independent information, in order to make themselves less reliant on the executive branch. Most important, they wanted their own budget so that they would not be left in the position of responding piecemeal to the President's unified budget.[19]

In 1974 the opponents of the imperial Presidency made up a fairly substantial portion of Congress, but the proponents of budget reform had an even broader constituency. Many fiscal conservatives concerned with budget deficits that occasionally reached into the tens of billions of dollars wanted to find a way to restrain the growth in government spending. They accepted budget reform, particularly the idea of a congressional budget, because they thought it would force greater restraint on the part of the members of Congress. Since the beginning of the nation, members of Congress had been free to vote in favor of individual appropriations bills and revenue bills without ever having to go on record in support of a deficit or surplus. Members of Congress never had to vote for a deficit. They could vote for low taxes and high expenditures, both of which were

---

19. See Kettl, *Deficit Politics,* 129–30.

popular with their constituents, without ever having to take responsibility for the resulting deficits. A congressional budget would force them to take responsibility for the bottom line and thereby promote greater fiscal responsibility.[20]

One other group was also enthusiastic about budget reform—programmatic liberals. A number of liberal members of Congress shared the Progressive belief that national policy was too often the outcome of competing private interests and compromises among those interests. Instead, policy should reflect a vision of the national interest. It should be a unified set of programs that represent a coherent and comprehensive national policy agenda. Programmatic liberals therefore signed on to budget reform because they thought the new congressional budget could become a major tool for establishing the nation's policy priorities.[21]

The Budget Act as passed addressed all these concerns. It placed strict limits on presidential impoundments. It created the Congressional Budget Office to provide Congress with its own independent source of information on the budget. It created budget committees in both the House and the Senate. These committees were charged with creating a congressional budget that would be adopted by Congress by May 1 of each year and that would establish limits and set priorities to be observed when Congress passed individual appropriations bills during the summer months. Any discrepancies between the budget resolution passed on May 1 and the individual appropriations bills would be ironed out in a second budget resolution to be passed by September 1. This second resolution became known as reconciliation.

With such wide-ranging appeal, it is remarkable that the budget process was such a dismal failure. In fact, while support may have come from a wide range of sources, the depth of support was not very great. From the beginning, the foundations of the budget process were shaky, and many members feared that the process would collapse before it had a chance to become established. The primary fear was that, when faced with limits that would threaten their individual pet projects, members would quickly revolt against the process. If the process were effective in restricting expenditures, it would almost certainly be doomed to failure because of the strong institutional incentives for members to continue the flow of bene-

20. Allen Schick notes the importance of the concern over excessive spending as a motive for conservative support for the Budget Act, but he also claims that from the beginning conservatives knew that the Act lacked sufficient strength to reduce spending. See Allen Schick, "The First Five Years of Congressional Budgeting," in *The Congressional Budget Process After Five Years,* ed. Rudolph G. Penner (Washington, D.C.: American Enterprise Institute, 1981), 3–34.

21. Ibid., 25.

fits to their districts. So from the beginning there was a tendency to defer substantive use of the budget process in the name of keeping the process alive. The budget committees were scrupulously careful not to set any ceilings on spending that might actually limit spending. Reports leaked out that members of the budget committees actually waited for word from the appropriations committees before establishing any ceilings on expenditures. The budget committees wanted to be sure they would do nothing to offend the powerful members of the appropriations committees.[22]

In some cases the process actually encouraged increased spending. Fearful that they might accidentally place too restrictive a ceiling on appropriations in a given area, the budget committees would tend to err on the side of generosity if they did not know specifically how much the appropriations committees would want to spend. Of course, when the appropriations committees learned that the budget committees had capped their spending at levels even higher than they had desired, they felt virtually obligated to increase their spending to the higher level.[23]

The Budget Act failed even more miserably with regard to agenda-setting. Each time a member of Congress suggested that an increase in spending in one area might require a cut in another area, a general retreat was sounded. Members of Congress went out of their way to say that in no way did they want their support for a particular pet project to be interpreted as hostility toward other spending programs.[24]

There was one way in which the reform of the budget-making process was a success. The Congressional Budget Office did provide Congress with an alternative source of information. In making its own budget calculations, it no longer had to rely on the executive branch for information. Even more important, Congress now had its own agency providing numbers that would generally support its own legislative preferences. But on the whole, the Budget Act did little else that it promised. Between 1975 and 1980, it had little perceptible effect on the outcome of the budget process.

Ironically the process became important only in the early years of the Reagan administration, when the congressional budget process helped limit spending and set national priorities, much in the manner envisioned for it. The irony was that the priorities and limits reflected the policy initiatives of Ronald Reagan and not those of Congress. Reagan had a unified perspective, and he was able to build a national constituency behind his budget priorities. The congressional budget process enabled him

22. Ibid., 19–23.
23. Ibid., 22.
24. Ibid., 25–28.

to translate that unified perspective and national constituency into concrete legislative action. Without the budget process, Reagan would have been forced to lobby piecemeal on numerous appropriations and revenue bills. He would not have been able to focus his lobbying effort on a single vote. He would have found it very difficult to mobilize his constituency to call and write their members of Congress for each of the individual pieces of legislation. He might have succeeded nonetheless, but it would have been more difficult and in all probability a more mixed success.[25]

Thus, not only did the congressional budget reform initially fail to limit spending and to set priorities, it ultimately failed in its primary objective: limiting presidential power. Instead, it aided the President in conducting the most massive shift in budget priorities since the New Deal.

After Reagan's initial success, the process ceased to serve any useful function. If anything, it served to thwart efficient action on the budget by Congress or by the President. Much debate remained focused on the budget resolution, but the resolution became increasingly irrelevant. For several years Congress failed to pass a second budget resolution as required under the Budget Act and eventually scrapped the second resolution altogether. The appropriations committees became less effective under the reformed process, often failing to pass appropriations bills. The government typically operated on continuing resolutions during the Reagan years. And then there were the deficits.[26]

RESPONDING TO THE DEFICIT PROBLEM

The extent of the deficit problem is debatable. What is a reasonable budget deficit? What are the effects of long-term deficits? How should the budget be calculated? The answers to each of these questions is anything but obvious.[27] In the later Reagan years, when political interest in the deficits was very high, the deficits as a percentage of the gross national product (GNP) were actually declining. At that time, they were running at 4 to 5 percent of GNP, nowhere near the 25 percent level in the last year of

25. For a discussion of Reagan's use of the budget process, see Shuman, *Politics and the Budget*, 256–66.

26. For an account of the stalemate, see Kettl, *Deficit Politics*, 131–36.

27. For a good account of the debate in Congress over the importance of deficits, see Steven E. Schier, *A Decade of Deficits: Congressional Thought and Fiscal Action* (Albany, N.Y.: SUNY Press, 1992), 19–52. See also Don Kettl's discussion entitled "Why Deficits Matter," in his *Deficit Politics*, 17–37.

World War II. The deficits were also coincident with one of the longest peacetime economic expansions in American history.

Arguments against the budget deficit have often been based on faulty premises. The most familiar refrain was a line the Democrats stole from anti–New Deal Republicans: Private individuals or businesses can't run deficits and continue to survive, so why should the federal government be able to do so? Of course, most individuals and businesses do borrow money. Capital investment is at the heart of capitalism. The real difference between the private sector and the federal government is that the private sector distinguishes between operating expenditures and capital expenditures, whereas the federal government does not. If the federal government were to copy the private sector in this respect, the budget deficit picture would look quite different, and it might be easier to determine what a realistic level of deficit spending would be. But there has been little interest in this type of reform.[28]

The actual reforms of the 1980s did little to improve the deficit picture. As we shall see, the most highly publicized reforms have been ineffective or pernicious. To the extent that any genuine progress has been made, it has come through the back door and has gone largely unnoticed.

To understand the problems and prospects of budget reform it is first useful to look at the two reform proposals. Both Reagan and Bush called for a line-item veto and a balanced-budget amendment as a way of fighting the deficits. Clinton has endorsed the idea of a line-item veto, and pressure continues to grow in Congress for passage of a balanced-budget amendment. However, neither reform has been adopted.[29] This is all to the good,

28. It is surprising that the proposal for a capital budget has received relatively little attention. Perhaps the fear is that it would be taken as an attempt to eliminate a large portion of the deficit by sleight of hand. It is true that a capital budget would make the deficit numbers look better immediately without changing any of the underlying dynamics of current fiscal policy. Its virtue, however, would be that it gives us a more realistic way to look at the budget. The switch to a capital budget was discussed at Clinton's economic summit, and such a change would certainly be consistent with Clinton's emphasis on government investment as opposed to government spending. But the fear that the change would be derided as a gimmick, and the difficulty in determining what should be considered a capital expenditure, may prevent further serious consideration.

29. In spring 1992 and in the face of a huge deficit, the complaints of Ross Perot, and a general level of dissatisfaction with Congress rarely equaled in American history, a balanced-budget amendment was again introduced and defeated. As this book goes to press, yet another vote is scheduled. At the beginning of his term, Clinton attempted to work out a deal with a Democratic Congress for an enhanced recision power. I think it is noteworthy that Clinton and Congress turned to the executive power of impoundment rather than the legislative power of the line-item veto in an attempt to reach a compromise. But interest in this proposal appears to have waned, and even if it is resurrected it will have little effect on the deficit.

because each of these reforms is inconsistent with the constitutional role of the President.

The line-item veto would probably have limited impact on the deficits. The major problems with the deficits are not back-door spending but major areas such as entitlement. In addition, the item veto might undermine consensus-building in Congress. The coalition-building process Congress uses to build support for legislation would be seriously threatened if the concessions that promoted compromise could be stripped from the legislation through a line-item veto. Moreover, Congress could avoid any responsibility for fiscal restraint because the final determination on individual items would be left to the President. These problems arise because the item veto would unconstitutionally insinuate the President into the legislative process. The President participates in the legislative process because of his unified perspective. He can present a unified proposal, and he can respond to a bill that he believes is on the whole undesirable. But as soon as the President fine-tunes legislation through an item veto, he assumes the role and responsibility of the members of Congress. A President can veto a piece of legislation, explaining that certain specific provisions are responsible for his decision. Congress can in turn choose whether to excise those provisions in exchange for presidential support or stick with the bill as written even if that means defeat. But a President can no more unilaterally excise specific provisions of the legislation than the Senate can negotiate or rewrite a treaty. The Senate can recommend changes in a treaty, but in the final analysis the Senate must accept or reject the treaty as a whole.[30]

The line-item veto is far more problematic than impoundment from the standpoint of the Constitution. Since Watergate and the impoundment restrictions passed by Congress in its wake, Presidents have been reluctant to claim a right to impound. They have sought the item veto as an alternative. However, they would be on far sounder ground claiming a right to impound funds than they are in seeking an item veto. As we shall see in the next chapter, impoundment rests on the assumption that once there is an independent executive such an executive will inevitably possess some discretion as to how programs are administered and how funds are actually spent. The assumption behind impoundment is that the question of how to spend appropriated funds may in some circumstances legitimately give rise to the question of whether funds should be expended at all. Much more needs to be said to defend this proposition, but the point here is

---

30. Treaties have the force of law but are not the same as law. They are negotiated by the President. The Senate can accept or reject the outcome of the President's efforts, but it can never negotiate a treaty itself.

merely that the case for impoundment rests on an identifiable element of executive power, whereas the item veto rests on a fundamental confusion of legislative and executive power.

It is likely that both Reagan and Bush knew Congress would never give them a line-item veto. It is even possible that they understood that the veto would have little positive effect on the deficit or the budget process in general. But politically it appeared to be too good an issue to pass up.[31] The call for the item veto allowed Bush and Reagan to identify themselves as supporters of deficit reduction without having to suggest any specific painful measures that might lead to genuine deficit reduction.

The balanced-budget amendment is also in large part a political red-herring. Clearly there are circumstances when a balanced budget is not a good idea. What would Ronald Reagan have done if there had been a balanced-budget amendment on the books in the early years of his administration? Would political circumstances have allowed him to cut domestic spending more than he did? Is it not more likely that he would have been pushed to raise taxes or cut defense spending, or some combination of the two? Reagan may have wanted a balanced budget, but without a balanced-budget amendment he was free to decide whether balancing the budget was as important as lowering taxes or increasing defense spending. Obviously, he decided it was not. To deny him the ability to make such a choice is to rob him of the discretion any executive must have to respond to a myriad of circumstances.

An additional problem with the balanced-budget amendment is that it attempts to guarantee a policy outcome through an institutional mechanism. Institutional mechanisms are good at providing incentives or disincentives for behavior, but they cannot guarantee a result. The attempt to do so reflects a Progressive belief that politics can be eliminated from government. Institutions can channel politics, but they are no substitute for politics. One cannot escape the need to debate priorities and to build consensus for priorities.

This is the reason a balanced-budget amendment would be unworkable. Any amendment would have to have an escape clause, and it would not be long before both Congress and the President would be playing Houdini. Even without an escape clause, the amendment is based on a faulty assumption—that the budget adequately captures and predicts reality. In the presence of a balanced-budget amendment, Congress need only re-

---

31. A more legitimate issue is raised by the passage of omnibus appropriations bills. Presidents might well complain that Congress is passing bills that include too many provisions relating to too many different issues. The solution, however, is a traditional veto of any bill the President deems to be too broad, not a line-item veto. The President should use the constitutional mechanism at his disposal rather than invent a new one.

define the budget to eliminate any deficit. There is ample precedent for this practice. Social Security, initially considered to be an off-budget item, was brought onto the budget by Lyndon Johnson because the surplus in the Social Security Trust Fund helped to mask the deficit. Even more common is the practice of summoning "rosy scenario" to cure our budget ills: Does it look like we will have a deficit? Don't worry. We only need to change our economic assumptions. Predict that unemployment will shrink from 7 percent to 4 percent, that interest rates will decline by 3 percent, that the GNP will grow by 10 percent, and that inflation will increase by 15 percent, and your budget deficit is a thing of the past. It doesn't matter that these are unreasonable assumptions. The point is that in important respects the budget is the product of guesswork. There is no way to establish a permanent objective standard by which to judge the accuracy of the guesses employed. In fact, some of Ronald Reagan's "rosy scenarios" turned out to be more accurate than the pessimistic forecasts of more respected experts.

A balanced-budget amendment cannot guarantee a balanced budget, because the budget will be held captive to uncertain economic variables. The budget is a guess—an educated guess perhaps, but nonetheless a guess. And because it is a guess, political actors will have every incentive to guess in a way that is consistent with their policy or political preferences.

Although the balanced-budget amendment got no further than the line-item veto, it did provide the inspiration for the reform that was adopted: the Gramm-Rudman-Hollins Act (GRH). GRH was superior to both the 1974 Congressional Budget Act and the balanced-budget amendment. Unlike the balanced-budget amendment it did not seek an immediate balanced budget or promise a balanced budget for ever after. It established a policy that would take gradual steps to reduce the deficit until it was eliminated. At that point the act would become a dead letter, and the normal policy process would be free to shape the budget.

Unlike the Congressional Budget Act, Gramm-Rudman-Hollins recognized that deficit reduction would require some means of enforcement, some powerful institutional incentive, if it was to be effective. The authors of GRH believed that they had created such a mechanism in the form of sequestration. The sequestration provision stated that if Congress failed to reduce the deficit by the required increment, then automatic across-the-board spending cuts would be implemented. Congress would be robbed of its discretion, and some favored programs would be faced with serious cuts. The prospect of sequestration was so devastating that Congress would never risk it.

In spite of these positive signs, GRH remained an ill-conceived reform. In GRH, Congress continued to try to have it both ways regarding enforcement. It included sequestration, but it placed sequestration under the control of the Comptroller-General, a legislative branch official. The idea of a legislative branch official having the ultimate responsibility for checking the legislature was not only impractical but, according to the Supreme Court in the *Synar* case, unconstitutional.[32] A legislative branch official cannot be charged with an essentially executive function. Following the *Synar* case, GRH was without any effective means of enforcement.

The *Synar* decision, however, turned out to be a blessing in disguise for supporters of the GRH process. Congress was forced to face up to the fact that if sequestration was to be meaningful it must be under the control of the executive branch. The second Gramm-Rudman Act (GR II) was passed in 1987. (Senator Hollins did not co-sponsor the 1987 bill, and the "GRH process" became the "GR process.") It turned control of sequestration over to the director of the Office of Management and Budget, an executive branch official. This enhancement of executive authority over the budget process occurred even though the Republicans had recently lost control of the Senate. Even more important was the fact that Gramm-Rudman II gave Congress an opportunity to rewrite the deficit targets of GRH.

By 1987 it was obvious that even the gradual reduction of the deficit that had been proposed was too optimistic. The first-year targets were so low that they were easily met. The second-year targets were reached by virtue of some one-time asset sales, some one-time "revenue enhancements" resulting from the transition rules of the 1986 tax reform act, and some genuine deficit-reduction measures. But without the first two factors, it was obvious that the original targets for the second year could not have been reached. The supposedly realistic and enforceable limits established by GRH thus proved to be unrealistic and easily avoided.

In 1990 the same scenario was replayed. The savings-and-loan bailout and a weak economy put the new targets beyond reach, and once again Congress was forced to punt on fourth down and long yardage. GR III was enacted establishing new and reduced deficit targets, but the belief that phased reduction of the deficits was realistic and enforceable under the GR process was quickly fading.

The reasons for the failure of Gramm-Rudman should be obvious. Most of the inherent difficulties of the balanced-budget amendment carry over to the Gramm-Rudman process. The desire for a balanced budget is one of many competing goals of budget policy, but there is ample evidence to suggest that it is not the highest priority with the executive branch, the legislative branch, or the people. Whether this is the result of shortsight-

---

32. *Bowsher v. Synar,* 478 U.S. 714 (1986).

edness, or whether it represents a reasonable assessment of national priorities, is irrelevant from the standpoint of the operation of Gramm-Rudman. The fact is that there is usually tremendous political pressure to place budget-balancing behind other goals.

It is also important to remember that even though Gramm-Rudman tried to make the goal of a balanced budget more realistic by creating a process of gradual deficit reduction, it did nothing to counter the fact that "the budget" is a very elastic concept. Transferring items on and off the budget and projecting rosy scenarios are political strategies that have been as effective under Gramm-Rudman as they would be under a balanced-budget amendment. What has also come to light under Gramm-Rudman is the effect of such manipulation. It encourages Congress to focus on measures that will improve the budget picture *this* year, regardless of the long-term effect of such decisions. Asset sales, for example, may improve the budget picture for the current fiscal year but mask a long-term problem. Given the structure of Gramm-Rudman, however, there is little incentive to look for long-term savings. The long term and the short term are too often punctuated by an election.

IS MEANINGFUL BUDGET REFORM POSSIBLE?

The budget process is in trouble, but it is a mistake to believe that reform of the process will solve all the problems surrounding the budget. In particular, it is a mistake to believe that any institutional reform will automatically eliminate the deficit. What institutional reform might do is lead to more-efficient development and implementation of an enforceable budget.

If we want to pursue constitutional budget reform, we should take our bearings from institutional capacities of the different branches. A more modest "budget amendment," rather than a balanced-budget amendment, might be successful if it met certain conditions: It should avoid the error of trying to guarantee policy outcomes through institutional reforms. It should not impose a fixed balanced-budget or deficit requirement. Instead, it should focus on real figures, such as expenditures and revenues, figures that Congress can control, rather than on projected deficits of dubious validity. It should guarantee that the budget is enforceable and passed early enough to get on with the other aspects of governing. Such a budget amendment would work because it would be based on an understanding of the distinctive constitutional roles of Congress and the President in the budgetary process. The proposed process would operate as follows:

1. The President submits budget by January 15.
2. By May 1, Congress approves the President's budget or passes its own by concurrent resolution.[33]
3. If Congress fails to act by this date, the President's budget takes effect.
4. Congress will pass appropriations bills consistent with the budget by September 1.
5. If an appropriations bill is passed in excess of the amounts provided for in the budget resolution, the President will be free to impound excess funds from the particular appropriations bill involved.
6. If a continuing resolution is passed in excess of the budget resolution, the President will be free to impound funds from any program within the continuing resolution to reach the levels required by the budget resolution.

The objections to this proposal are easily predicted. The primary objection is that it gives too much power to the President. But Congress can pass its own budget. Impoundment would then take place only when Congress ignored its own self-imposed limits. The President's budget would be implemented only when Congress was unable to do its job. Even when the impoundment process is triggered, however, the President might be constrained by political pressures.

The virtue of the system is that it ensures responsibility and encourages action. The President will submit a budget. He has a strong incentive to be realistic because he might ultimately have the power to enforce this budget. He will try to make his budget as attractive as possible to Congress, so that Congress will be less tempted to pass one of its own. On the other hand, Congress will be encouraged to pass its own budget. The members will know that the alternative is not inaction but the adoption of the President's budget. Moreover, they will see that whatever budget is adopted, there is a greater likelihood that it will be enforced. The provisions for a blanket impoundment power in the event of a continuing resolution will encourage the passage of individual appropriations bills.

Could each branch avoid action in this system? The answer is yes. Congress could avoid action and turn the problem over to the President. The President could ignore the budget resolution and fail to impound. But

33. I propose use of a concurrent resolution because it would be more consistent with current practice. A more radical step would be to make the budget resolution a joint resolution requiring the President's signature. This would provide a more powerful incentive for action, but it would also give rise to even greater objections on the grounds that it would grant too much power to the President.

responsibility for inaction would be more clearly fixed. It is unlikely that both branches will pass up the opportunity to use the budget resolution as a means of establishing their priorities. The system takes advantage of the constitutional separation of powers. It ensures recognition of the different constitutional perspectives, and it uses those different perspectives as a way to encourage action, taking advantage of the President's role as a policy initiator and his role in the implementation of policy.

Although there is a tendency to say that Congress will never go along, some steps in this direction have already been taken. Initially Congress was reluctant to give the power over sequestration to the executive branch, but it soon recognized, with the help of the Supreme Court, that there was no workable alternative. The logic of the Constitution prevailed in this case, and it continues to prevail in others.

GR III provides even more dramatic evidence that Congress might approve this kind of reform. The revision of the deficit targets may have been the least important part of the legislation. Although the tax increases certainly contributed to George Bush's defeat, they too are relatively insignificant in terms of overall budget policy. What is significant are the changes in the budget process that OMB Director Richard Darman managed to slip in by the back door.

Darman followed the spirit of the Constitution in his proposals for budget reform. He deemphasized deficit targets in favor of spending targets. Darman created caps on three categories of spending for a five-year period and placed other spending on a pay-as-you-go basis. This focuses the process on real rather than hypothetical numbers. He reduced congressional discretion and increased executive discretion in pursuit of deficit reduction by giving the Office of Management and Budget greater control of the power to sequester during this five-year period. Moreover, the spending targets provided greater restraints on the natural inclinations of Congress than they did on those of the executive. The defense targets were not a problem, being consistent with the general drift of policy. The domestic limits were also consistent with the desire to limit the tendency of Congress to distribute more goods, while still maintaining discretion for necessary spending if other cuts or sources of revenue could be identified.[34]

Darman's budget deal was temporary, and the principles underlying it have not received much support from the Clinton administration. However, it has influenced the budget process much longer than many thought it would, even though Congress was faced with the pressures to increase

---

34. For a discussion of the importance of these reforms in the process, see Shuman, *Politics and the Budget*, 330–41.

spending to counter the recession and the desire to shift the savings from deeper defense cuts to domestic programs. It has served as a baseline for congressional criticism (both Democratic and Republican) of Clinton's spending proposals. The political fire that Darman drew from both the right and the left is undoubtedly a tribute to the short-term success of his efforts.[35] If and when concern over long-term budget deficits provides sufficient impetus for real action, Darman's temporary deal may be a starting point for genuine reform. Indeed, the debate over caps on entitlement spending is similar to Darman's approach. In any event, through Darman's deal Congress had at least temporarily backed into a reform that gives greater institutional control over the budget to the President. And it is only through such reform that the budget process is likely to become more unified.[36]

POPULAR LEADERSHIP, LEGISLATIVE LEADERSHIP, AND THE BUDGET

Even if major reform of the budget process does not occur, the President's unified national perspective will continue to allow him to set the terms of the budget debate. It is not clear whether we will see renewed efforts to address the deficit problem in the coming years, or whether the deficit will be forced to take a back seat to other political goals. But what is clear is that the answer to that question will be influenced more by the President's agenda than by any other single factor. Congress inevitably makes changes in the President's budget agenda, even when the President and Congress are controlled by the same party. But those changes will take place within a framework established by the President.

In the 1980s Congress often claimed that the President's budget was

35. The source of the conservative criticism is obvious. Darman gave in on a key element of the Reagan Revolution—no new taxes. But the conservatives either failed to see that the spending limits could have a genuine effect on the deficit, or they had moved from indifference on the deficit issue to an outright hostility to any genuine effort at deficit reduction. Liberals, on the other hand, were so busy reveling in the partisan advantage gained by having Bush break his tax pledge that they did not focus on the procedural changes until those changes started to limit their desire to increase domestic spending and shift funds from defense to domestic spending.

36. One major defect of the budget agreement should not be overlooked: the failure of President Bush to explain it adequately to the American people. For an excellent discussion of this failure, see Terry Eastland, *Energy in the Executive: The Case for the Strong Presidency* (New York: The Free Press, 1992), 49–63.

dead on arrival, but even these so-called DOA budgets greatly determined the shape of the final budget; the President's budgets may have been wounded but they weren't killed. The kind of changes Congress made represented little more than the kind of adjustments that were typical before the establishment of the congressional budget process and would be typical if it were abandoned. In the final analysis, Congress has not taken control of the budget agenda since 1980. Its major goal through much of that period—a tax increase—is something it would not dare pursue without presidential backing. Only when the President was ready to raise taxes in 1991 did he "reluctantly" submit a unified plan that included a tax increase. Congress did not give Reagan or Bush everything they wanted, and often gave them things they did not want, but it would be difficult to argue that Congress set the terms of the budget debate.

It is to his credit that, as President, Bill Clinton has generally avoided an appeal to institutional gimmicks as a panacea for the deficit problem. He has forthrightly claimed that there is no substitute for strong leadership and tough choices. But there is reason to suspect that his tough leadership on the deficit issue may prove to be inadequate in the long run. By his own projections, the deficit will be increasing again in five years. Clinton has also taken advantage of the amorphous quality of the budget to create a greater perception of change than is warranted by economic and political realities.

Clinton frequently criticized Reagan and Bush for using "rosy scenarios" to paint a brighter picture of the deficit than was warranted at the time. But Clinton has adopted the opposite strategy. He has used the most pessimistic numbers possible in order to exaggerate his claims of deficit reduction. Clinton does not measure his deficit reduction package by the extent to which it will reduce the deficit from its present level. Instead, he posits a hypothetical baseline deficit that shows what the deficit would have been had he not acted. But that baseline deficit ignores the effects of the 1990 budget agreement and claims credit for renewing other deficit reduction measures that have been renewed automatically for years.[37]

In July 1993 Clinton was pressured into releasing new deficit projections that showed that his original estimate of the Fiscal Year 1993 deficit was $37 billion too high. Nonetheless, he claimed that this miscalculation should cast no doubt on his projections for subsequent years. To recognize that the deficit was declining before the adoption of his economic plan would undercut his ability to claim credit for any future improvement in the deficit picture. He must cling to the most negative possible

37. For a concise discussion of Clinton's budget manipulations, see Tim Muris, "Budget Manipulations," *American Enterprise* 4 (May–June 1993), 24–28.

estimates of future deficits until his plan takes effect and he can claim that the reduction in the deficit is a direct result of his actions. But in adopting this strategy, Clinton is as guilty of budget manipulation as his predecessors. Although he has not sought salvation in quick institutional fixes, he has demonstrated more concern with the perception of leadership than with genuine leadership.

Most analysts now agree that any successful attempt to deal with long-term structural deficits must address the issue of entitlements, but Clinton has made only the most tentative steps at addressing this problem. He claims that his health-care reform proposal will have a substantial impact on entitlement spending, but that claim is at best highly speculative.[38] His emphasis on taxing the rich and cutting defense hardly constitutes bold leadership. In fact, given the elimination of the BTU tax, the failure of the economic stimulus package, and the congressional pressure to add more spending cuts to Clinton's initial package, there is good reason to question Clinton's responsibility for the final plan.

Whether or not one believes that the final budget departed significantly from Clinton's initial proposals, Clinton will be held accountable for its effects. Bush understood his agreement to raise taxes in 1990 to be reluctant compromise. He agreed to the tax increase only in order to get congressional support for a final budget. But regardless of his reluctance to raise taxes, the 1990 Budget Agreement became Bush's budget agreement. When the economy turned sour, it turned sour as a result of Bush's budget policy. Bush learned an important lesson: Members of Congress can hide in the crowd, but the President must take responsibility. Certainly Bush could justly claim that he was given too much responsibility for a budget passed by a Democratic Congress. But it should have come as no surprise to Bush that under the separation of powers system the President is most easily called to account for national policy.

We will better appreciate the complex character of political responsibility if we understand the constitutional functions of the executive and legislature in the policy-making process. Foreign policy is more clearly executive in that it is derived from a series of actions. The only legal framework is found in treaties negotiated, interpreted, enforced, and abrogated by the executive. But domestic policy is codified in law. The law represents a fixed statement of policy. The law also represents a statement of consensus among the various interests represented in the legislature. It gives definition to policy and provides general rules for the implementation of policy.

38. Entitlement spending increased from 28.3 percent of the budget in 1962 to 50.3 percent of the budget in 1993. Between 1991 and 1992, medicaid expenditures increased at a rate of 31.5 percent. See George Hager, "Entitlements: The Untouchable May Become Unavoidable" *Congressional Quarterly Weekly Report*, January 2, 1993, 22–30.

Domestic policy is conducted within the parameters established by law. The consensus reflected in law provides support and legitimacy for policy. Thus, the essence of domestic policy is law passed by the legislature.

The role of Congress is particularly important with regard to budget policy. Congress was assigned control of the purse strings. No money was to be spent except in pursuance of a legal appropriation. Tax bills were to be initiated in the House. The evidence does appear to support the primacy of the legislature with regard to budgetary matters.

There is reason to question whether the congressional role in the budget process has not dramatically changed with the general growth in government activity. Primacy was given to Congress because the Founders thought that closeness to the people would lead the Congress to be protective of the people's interests. Therefore, they assumed that Congress would be reluctant to pass high taxes and would maintain a limited government. Today's Congress seems to be more prone to expand expenditures. However, the major change is not in the character of Congress but in the character of government as a whole. In an era when government provides benefits to individual interests, it is not surprising that Congressmen would see their role as protecting the interests of their constituencies in receiving benefits. The pursuit of pork is consistent with the constitutional function of Congress—the protection of the interests of particular constituencies.

The President, however, also plays an important role in the policy process. Control over the implementation of policy allows the President to affect policy. As we shall see in the next chapter, laws define and create pools of executive discretion. The executive is limited, but within limits he can refine the definition of policy. Laws frequently create conflicting goals or claims, and the President must at least make a choice of emphasis among these claims. The veto power is also important. The President can block legislative action, and the threat of a veto can give the President a voice in law-making and policy-making.

The most important role, however, is the President's role as a policy initiator. Article II, Section 3, of the Constitution calls on the President to make recommendations based on his view of the state of the union. The President can make recommendations from a unified perspective. As noted in Chapter 2, the Constitutional Convention required this rather than recommended it, in order to avoid presidential reticence. This provision confers influence and not power. The President cannot pass legislation, but he is clearly in the best position to set the legislative agenda. As we have seen, historical practice supports this view. Policy initiatives have been primarily presidential. Congress has refined and defined policy and has built consensus. It has operated between the broad statement of principles of policy enunciated by the President and the detailed implementation by the executive.[39] It has acted to codify policy and provide a framework for implementation.

The 1986 Tax Reform Act provides a good example. It might be argued that the idea was initiated in Congress, but as a congressional initiative it went nowhere. It became a serious item of debate only when the President took the initiative to gather support for the general principle of tax reform. Once support for the general principle was established, Congress had to build consensus around the specific provisions of the law. The President had little power, but his influence was absolutely crucial to the change in policy.[40]

Because of the democratic base of the constitutional President, the least authoritative power may lead to one of the most important presidential functions. The President has a unique claim to represent national public opinion as the only officer who can look at the budget as a whole from a national perspective. A proposal for restructuring the budget priorities of the nation will prove to be successful only if it has the political influence of the President behind it.[41]

Through an examination of budget reforms and proposals for reform, we have been forced to reconsider assumptions that are frequently made about the character of the policy-making process. Many of those assumptions are wrong. The myth of the modern Presidency is in error when it ignores the importance of the President's *constitutional* role as popular leader and legislative agenda setter. That error leads us to misunderstand the present and the past.

The nineteenth century was not a period of major congressional policy initiatives. Budget priorities changed only when the partisan alignment changed, and partisan realignment in the nineteenth century was the product of presidential leadership.[42] When we look back to the nineteenth cen-

39. In the literature on party realignment, this refinement of policy may be identified with the theory of secular as opposed to critical realignment. See V. O. Key Jr., "Secular Realignment and the Party System," *Journal of Politics* 21 (May 1959), 159.

40. For a discussion of the passage of the Tax Reform Act, see Jeffrey H. Birnbaum and Alan S. Murray, *Showdown at Gucci Gulch* (New York: Random House, 1987).

41. In late spring 1992 three Republican and three Democratic Senators appeared on ABC's "Nightline" to propose a format in which each of the three presidential candidates would be asked to respond to detailed questions about their proposals to address the deficit problem. Ted Koppel asked the obvious question: why these six Senate leaders did not simply formulate their own bipartisan plan. The response was that no plan would be successful without presidential leadership.

42. In the realignment literature there is some reluctance to admit this point. Commentators such as Ladd (*American Political Parties*) tend to identify the causes of realignment with social and economic change. James Sundquist focuses more on political issues and the

tury, we do not look to Congress for the major shifts in policy. Just as we do today, we look to particular Presidents to mark a new direction for the government. Washington, Jefferson, Jackson, and Lincoln are the pivotal figures for national policy in the nineteenth century. Even at the end of the nineteenth century the major shifts in policy are tied to particular Presidents: the end of reconstruction, to Hayes; the attempt to restrict the growth of government spending, especially spending on veterans benefits, to Cleveland; the resurgence of the Republican party, to McKinley.

Congress did play a major policy-making role, just as it does today. And some recent scholars have suggested that the myth of the modern Presidency not only depreciates presidential leadership in the nineteenth century but also exaggerates the President's success as legislative leader today. No President succeeds with all his initiatives, and Congress significantly refines and alters most programs submitted by the President.[43] In the nineteenth century, Congress adjusted and refined the existing policy agenda, just as it does today. It worked out the details of tariff policy and spending policy within the framework created by the *Jeffersonian* Republicans, the *Jacksonian* Democrats, and the *Lincoln* Republicans. We see this not only with regard to budget policy but also in the case of slavery. The congressional giants of the nineteenth century—John Calhoun, Henry Clay, and Daniel Webster—achieved much of their fame for their role in the slavery debate. But even here we should remember that Congress was attempting to maintain consensus through compromise and refinement of the existing policy. Congress ultimately failed, and it took the presidential initiative of Lincoln to resolve the issue.[44]

Presidential initiatives were limited in the nineteenth century because

---

importance of leadership, but even he hesitates to speak simply of presidential leadership. See James Sundquist, *Dynamics of the Party System* (Washington, D.C.: The Brookings Institution, 1983). However, when specific realignments are discussed they are virtually always discussed in connection with a change in party dominance at the presidential level. The most important party leaders from the standpoint of realignment have almost universally been Presidents. The Jeffersonian Republicans, the Jacksonian Democrats, the rise of the Republican party under Lincoln, and the reassertion of Republican dominance in the election of McKinley all demonstrate the centrality of the Presidency to the phenomenon of realignment. There has never been a partisan realignment that was congressionally driven.

43. Bond and Fleisher provide a quantitative analysis of presidential success in controlling the legislative agenda. They conclude that even Presidents who enjoy a reputation for skillful legislative leadership are seriously limited in their ability to control the legislative agenda. Jon R. Bond and Richard Fleisher, *The President in the Legislative Arena* (Chicago: University of Chicago Press, 1990), esp. 220–40.

44. Sundquist, *Dynamics of the Party System*, 50–73.

government activity was generally limited. In an era when policy was mainly a matter of compromise and refinement of the existing framework, it is not surprising that Congress would appear to be the dominant branch. But it would be a mistake to assume that Congress ever consistently played the dominant role in policy *initiation*. When new policy directions were initiated, and when the consensus had to be redefined, it was presidential leadership that dominated the system.[45]

The President's twentieth-century role in the policy process is not an illegitimate infringement on legislative prerogatives. The Constitution created institutional incentives and structures that would lead to an important role for the President in the policy-making process. The President's role in domestic policy-making stems from two sources: his exercise of discretionary authority in the implementation of policy, which will be discussed in Chapter 4, and the political influence based on his constitutional position as the only unified popularly elected national officer. The President does not have the discretionary constitutional authority the legislature has—the authority to pass laws. And although his ability to present a unified plan does not confer discretionary authority, it does give him an advantage as an agenda setter. This advantage is reenforced by the political influence gained through popular national election—an important if sometimes fragile source of power in a system of popular government.[46]

With or without reform, the President is likely to continue to play an agenda-setting role in budget policy and in domestic policy generally. He will play that role more effectively if we understand the constitutional character and legitimacy of that role. We may also lessen our cynicism

45. This argument is not meant to suggest that Presidents in the nineteenth century drafted as much legislation or actively lobbied for as many bills as those in the twentieth century. In the twentieth century more issues have attracted presidential attention, and a large staff has been developed to promote the President's legislative agenda. But much of this change merely reflects the broader growth of government activity. My point is that in the nineteenth century major shifts in the direction or framework of the legislative agenda were led by the President, just as they are today.

46. The recent criticism of the rhetorical Presidency correctly identifies the dangers of an excessive reliance on rhetoric, but (as argued in Chapter 2) this literature also understates the importance of the President's rhetorical role. Presidents have always attempted to sway public opinion. The question is not whether a President will engage in popular leadership, but how. If Presidents have changed their rhetorical strategy over the years, such change does not inevitably suggest a transformation of the office. As Terry Eastland explains, the rhetorical strategy of the Presidency must inevitably change in order to deal with other social and technological changes. See Terry Eastland, *Energy in the Executive*, 26–27. We must be careful to distinguish between changes that represent necessary adaptations to social and technological change and changes that radically alter the office.

regarding Congress if we recognize that it was designed to represent competing interests and not as the source of unified policy initiatives. Only when we learn to recognize the distinctive types of power and influence created by the constitutional separation of powers will we be able to understand the potentials and problems of the policy-making process.[47]

47. Although some commentators have argued that the different perspectives of Congress and the Presidency are responsible for the gridlock that has created the current deficit, Morris Fiorina argues that other factors are more important. In fact, under unified government, he says, it is likely that the deficit would have been larger. See Morris Fiorina, *Divided Government* (New York: Macmillan Co., 1992), 92–96.

CHAPTER FOUR

Administrative Responsibility

According to the myth of the modern Presidency, another crucial change in the office has been the rise of an extensive bureaucracy in the White House to support the President's legislative agenda and independent policy-making. In one sense, the truth of the myth is obvious: the White House staff has mushroomed since Franklin Roosevelt took office. But the important question is whether this growth represents a substantial change in the character of the office.

The reason for the concern over the growth of the White House staff is that this staff exists explicitly to serve the President. While the primary function of the administrators in the cabinet departments is to carry out the laws, the function of the White House staff is not so easily defined by the principles of the rule of law. The creation of an independent staff to serve the President rests on the assumption that the President needs help in performing functions that go beyond mere execution of the law. We have often heard the rhetorical question "Do we have a government of laws or a government of 'men'?" The myth of the modern Presidency suggests that while the Constitution supported a limited office constrained by the principles of the rule of law, the reality of the modern Presidency has been the growth of extralegal executive discretion.

But the myth is incorrect because it fails to recognize that the conflict between legal and discretionary administrative authority goes back to the earliest days of the Constitution. Throughout our history there has been a conflict between the President and Congress over the question of who controls the bureaucracy. Administration is at the intersection of executive and legislative power. Administrators carry out the laws and therefore serve Congress. However, the reason for the creation of an independent executive is that the administration of laws requires discretion. The President's ability to direct the bureaucracy rests on the existence of a sphere of administrative discretion. The problem of administrative responsibility is to find a way to resolve the competing claims of the legislature and the executive, the competing claims of law and "men," while at the same time creating clear-cut lines of responsibility.

We can explore the issue of administrative responsibility by examining two case studies: the removal controversy and the rise and decline of the legislative veto. In both cases we shall see that Congress has made numerous attempts to gain tighter control over administration, but most attempts have ultimately failed. The Tenure of Office Act was not very effective. Civil service reform and the rise of independent regulatory commissions called into question the power of the President to control the bureaucracy. Both types of reforms placed limits on the executive's removal power, but neither moved in the direction of legislative control. Finally, the legislative veto was eventually declared unconstitutional. Given the failure of Congress to assert control, two fears have arisen: first, that the executive has usurped an important Congressional prerogative; second, that the bureaucracy of the administrative state may not be susceptible to control from either the executive or the legislative branches.

To understand the problem of administrative responsibility better, we must recognize that the administrative state is not at odds with the separation of powers. Modern liberal government has from its inception been administrative in character. The problem has been to reconcile the administrative state with the principle of consent. The U.S. Constitution does this by creating a legislature whose laws circumscribe the operation of the administrative state, and by creating an executive with an independent popular base who is responsible for the discretionary aspects of administration. Thus, an efficient, effective, and responsible operation of the administrative state depends on an adequate understanding of the separation of powers.

THE REMOVAL CONTROVERSY

The removal controversy culminated in the establishment of an independent executive power over administrators, but there is no explicit constitutional provision granting the removal power to the President. There was no discussion of the issue at the Constitutional Convention, and in the *Federalist* Hamilton said that the removal power should be shared with the Senate.[1] In the first Congress, however, Madison argued for the right of the executive alone to remove, claiming that without such power the President could not be held accountable for the conduct of the administration.[2]

Two controversies during Andrew Jackson's administration reopened the debate. Although *Kendall v. U.S.* was not decided until 1838 and did not directly address the issue of removal, it did represent an important victory for Congress in its battle with Jackson over the control of administrators. Stockton & Stokes had contracted with the U.S. government to carry the mail. When it came time to be paid, the Jackson administration was unwilling to do so. It seems that the owners of Stockton & Stokes were political opponents of Jackson and there was some question about the value of their services. Congress believed the contractor should get its money, so it passed an act saying that the Postmaster should pay them whatever amount the solicitor of the Post Office department deemed to be reasonable. The solicitor told Postmaster Amos Kendall that the firm should be paid $161,563, but Kendall, with Jackson's backing, refused to pay more than $122,102. Stockton & Stokes then turned to the courts seeking a writ of mandamus ordering payment of the full amount.[3]

The Supreme Court decided that it could issue a writ ordering full payment. The majority opinion stated that this order in no way represented interference on the part of the legislature or the judiciary in the affairs of the executive branch. The writ sought only to enforce a ministerial duty that neither the President nor the Postmaster had any authority to deny or control. The President cannot escape the expressed desires of the legislature by appealing to some notion of discretionary executive authority. Congress appeared to have won a major victory against the growth of executive power.[4]

In many ways, however, the case points to an emerging constitutional rationale for executive discretion in administrative matters. First, the Court admitted that there might be cases where the rights and powers of the executive would preclude judicial or legislative interference. The Kendall case was said to involve a mere ministerial function, but the Court,

1. In *Federalist* No. 77 Hamilton says explicitly: "The consent of [the Senate] would be necessary to displace as well as to appoint" (Alexander Hamilton et al., *The Federalist,* ed. Jacob E. Cooke [Cleveland: Meridian Books, 1961], 515).

2. *Annals of Congress,* 1789, 515–16, 519. See also Madison's "Letter to Edmund Pendleton," June 21, 1789, in *The Papers of James Madison,* ed. Charles F. Hobson and Robert Rutland (Charlottesville: University of Virginia Press, 1979), 12, 251–53.

3. *Kendall v. U.S.,* 37 U.S. (12 Pet.) 524 (1838).

4. Corwin identifies this case as an unambiguous victory for Congress. See Edward S. Corwin, *The President: Office and Powers* (New York: New York University Press, 1957), 84–85.

following in the tradition of *Marbury v. Madison*, clearly sanctioned the idea of an independent sphere of executive authority.[5]

Second, there is good reason to believe that the Supreme Court erred in its application of the distinction between ministerial and executive acts in this case. After all, Congress did not tell the Postmaster what Stockton & Stokes should be paid. It said in its legislation that the firm should be paid whatever the solicitor of the Post Office department thought was reasonable. Why didn't Congress simply determine the appropriate amount? The only possible reason is that it did not believe it was a question that could be decided by the legislature. By assigning the task to the solicitor, an executive branch official, Congress was tacitly admitting that such a decision should be handled by the executive branch, not the legislative branch. It was admitting that the task required the exercise of executive discretion. It required the experience and expertise that executive branch officials have. It was because Congress was not suited to making this type of decision that an independent executive branch was created. Congress was not designed to deal with individual cases.

Finally, the Court does not deal with the question of removal. What would the Court have said if Jackson had simply removed the solicitor and appointed one who would agree with him about the proper amount of payment? Jackson had done precisely that during another major controversy.

The removal controversy was the most important of Jackson's administration. It is, however, necessary to distinguish between two aspects of the removal controversy, or, to be more precise, between the two "removals" that made up the removal controversy. The first revolved around Jackson's decision to remove the deposits of the U.S. government from the National Bank. Jackson had already successfully vetoed legislation rechartering the Bank, but he feared that it might be resurrected in the future. The existing charter still had two years to run, and Jackson believed that he must take action to kill the Bank immediately, rather than wait for its charter to run out. He determined that the best method of execution would be to remove the deposits of the government.

Jackson claimed that as the chief executive officer of the government he had the right to determine where the funds of the government should be held. Congress had even given the Secretary of the Treasury explicit authorization to remove the funds from the Bank, if he determined that

5. In *Marbury v. Madison*, 5 U.S. (1 Cranch) 137 (1803), Justice John Marshall identified "political powers" of the President as where he may "use his own discretion, and is accountable only to his country." Although Corwin emphasizes that the Court had determined there was no room for political discretion in this case, he neglects the Court's reaffirmation of the existence of discretionary executive authority (Corwin, *The President*, 85).

they were unsafe. Jackson therefore ordered his Treasury Secretary to remove the government's money. This is where the second part of the "removal" controversy began. Jackson's Treasury Secretary, William Duane, refused to follow his instructions, claiming that he did not think the funds were unsafe. It was to him and not to Jackson that the discretion was given, and he concluded he must exercise that discretion by his own lights.[6]

After several attempts at persuasion, Jackson fired Duane. He succeeded in removing the funds only when he made a recess appointment of Roger B. Taney, his Attorney General, as Secretary of the Treasury. The Senate was outraged. Not only were the Senators appalled by Jackson's blatant attempt to kill the Bank, they were equally infuriated that Jackson had acted unilaterally in removing a cabinet officer. Although Madison had asserted the President's right to do so in the first Congress, most Presidents had managed to finesse the issue either by obtaining the resignation of the cabinet officer or by gaining Senate approval of a new cabinet-level secretary and therefore tacit approval for the removal.[7]

Jackson defended his action, relying heavily on Madison's earlier arguments.[8] Jackson claimed that the Senate's participation in the appointment process was an exception to the general principle of executive control of the bureaucracy. With the exception of the qualifications specifically enumerated in the Constitution, the President's control of the executive branch was to be understood as absolute. It would be absurd, he argued, to force a President to continue to serve with a cabinet officer in whom he had lost confidence. To do so would eliminate the President's ability to control the executive officials for whom he was politically responsible.

In response, Webster turned to Hamilton's argument for a shared power

6. For a discussion of the removal of the Treasury Secretary, see William S. Duane, "Dismissal of the Secretary of the Treasury," in *The Age of Jackson*, ed. Robert Remini (Columbia: University of South Carolina Press, 1972), 106–10. See also Robert Remini, *Andrew Jackson and the Bank War* (New York: Twayne, 1967); Robert Remini, "The Jackson Era," in *The Constitution and the American Presidency*, ed. Martin Fausold and Alan Shank (Albany, N.Y.: SUNY Press, 1991).

7. Remini, "The Jackson Era," 33–34.

8. Jackson argued in his "Protest": "Thus it was settled by the Constitution, the laws, and the whole practice of the government that the entire executive power is vested in the President of the United States; that as incident to that power [is] the right of appointing and removing those officers who are to aid him in the execution of the laws . . . ; that the custody of the public property and money is an executive function which . . . has always been exercised through the Secretary of the Treasury and his subordinates; that in the performance of his duties he is subject to the supervision and control of the President." For his complete argument, see the "Protest" in James D. Richardson, *A Compilation of the Messages and Papers of the Presidents*, 20 vols. (New York: Bureau of National Literature, 1897), 3:1288–313.

of removal. Webster argued that if the power of appointment was shared it followed logically that the power of removal should also be shared. Even more important to Webster, however, was his assumption that in our constitutional system the legislature should be supreme. If we were to have a limited constitutional government, the laws, not the will of the executive, must govern. To leave such discretion in the hands of the executive would be tantamount to giving him absolute control over the executive branch and eventually over the government as a whole.[9]

Neither Jackson nor Webster fully appreciated the complexity of the constitutional separation of powers. In defending his executive prerogatives, Jackson gave scant attention to the legitimate role of the legislature or to any limits on the exercise of executive authority. But in this case he clearly had the better of the argument with Webster. There is a difference between appointment and removal. Senate participation in appointment does not force the President to serve with a cabinet official he does not want; participation in the removal power could have such an effect. Such participation would therefore be an unconstitutional infringement on the President's legitimate sphere of authority, as Madison had argued earlier. Moreover, Jackson understood that legislative supremacy was not the doctrine animating the Constitution. The separation of powers was dependent on the creation and maintenance of an independent sphere of executive authority.[10]

In principle and in practice, Jackson had the better of the argument. Both his removal of the deposits and his removal of the Treasury Secretary stood, but doubts remained in the minds of the Whig members of Congress. Jackson was censured for his actions by the Senate, but after the Democratic victory in 1836 the censure was expunged from the Congressional Record.

The strongest assertion of legislative control over the cabinet came in the aftermath of the Civil War and Lincoln's assassination. Andrew Johnson's pursuit of a "moderate" Reconstruction policy along with his Southern background almost immediately placed him at odds with the Republicans in Congress and many members of his inherited cabinet.[11] Leading

---

9. "Webster's Reply to the 'Protest,'" in Remini, ed., *Age of Jackson*, 120–21.

10. Remini sees Jackson's actions as a break with established constitutional precedent, but they would be better understood as a fulfillment of the Constitution's potential (Remini, "The Jackson Era"). Although Jackson's predecessors were less active than Jackson, Jackson clearly draws on the arguments of the Founders and the potential for presidential power and influence created by the Constitution.

11. For a discussion of Johnson's Reconstruction policy, see Albert Castel, *The Presidency of Andrew Johnson* (Lawrence: University Press of Kansas, 1979).

Republicans tried to convince Johnson he should sit back and allow the cabinet to govern, but he resisted any such attempts to transfer political power from the office of the Presidency.

Sensing his hostility, Republicans in Congress passed the Tenure of Office Act in order to ensure that the radical Republicans maintained a foothold in the executive branch. The Tenure of Office Act required that Johnson obtain Senate approval before removing any cabinet officer or other presidential appointee. As long as Republicans hostile to Johnson's policies occupied key cabinet positions, there was hope that Johnson's policies could be circumvented and a more radical reconstruction policy pursued.

Andrew Johnson at first tried to work with the existing cabinet, but he soon recognized that this would lead to a complete usurpation of his authority as President. He therefore removed the most radical member of the cabinet, his Secretary of War. Congress refused to bow to Johnson's assertion of authority, and impeachment proceedings were initiated. Articles of impeachment were voted by the House, and a trial was conducted in the Senate.[12] A majority of the Senate voted for removal, but the vote was one short of the two-thirds majority required by the Constitution. Johnson held onto his office by a single vote.

It is hard to argue that this in any way marks a high point for presidential authority. Johnson's narrow escape from removal, and his inability to deal effectively with Congress or even his own cabinet, are usually taken as ample evidence of the failure of his Presidency.[13] But from another perspective, we may see this episode as an example of the strength of the constitutional office. What President has ever or will ever face greater threats to the authority of his office? Johnson assumed the office in the shadow of our greatest President and was bound to suffer from the comparison. His task was in some ways more difficult than Lincoln's. Lincoln had saved the Union, in the sense that he had preserved the parts of the Union, but Johnson was left with the task of reassembling those parts in the aftermath of civil war. Although he had always been on the side of the victors, suspicion of his innate Southern sympathies was sufficient to place the powers of any President under siege. And in the final analysis Johnson's policies lost any moral force as they degenerated into a simple

12. Johnson claimed that the Tenure of Office Act was unconstitutional, but he also argued that because Stanton was appointed by Lincoln, and not by himself, Stanton was not covered by the act. See Richard Pious, *The American Presidency* (New York: Basic Books, 1979), 72–75.

13. Richard Pious argues that it would be "absurd to contend that Johnson's acquittal strengthened the Presidency." By the end of his administration "Congressional supremacy" had been established. See ibid., 74.

defense of states' rights. Johnson did not even have the legitimacy of a popularly elected President, having gained the office as a result of assassination.[14]

If it were not for the strength of the office, and the constitutional supports for its independence, Johnson's personal failure might have extended to the failure of the office and the government as a whole. At the end of the battle, however, Johnson was in office and his Secretary of War was out. Cabinet government had not replaced presidential leadership, and Congress had not been able to take control of the executive branch through the cabinet. The super majority required by the Constitution for removal had given Johnson just enough institutional strength to stand against popular majorities in Congress. The President's constitutional position at the head of the executive branch was sufficiently well established that no member of the cabinet or any combination of members could stage a successful coup. More to the point, Congress could not take charge of the executive branch because it could never appoint its own cabinet, nor as it turned out could it effectively prevent removal.

The Tenure of Office Act remained on the books for many years, although it was weakened during Grant's administration.[15] But the courts did not address the removal question until 1926 in the case of *Myers v. U.S.* Myers had served as postmaster of Portland, Oregon, for several years, but in an effort to redistribute spoils the Democratic party under Woodrow Wilson ordered Myers's removal. Rather than go quietly, Myers protested, claiming that by statute the President could not remove a postmaster without the approval of the Senate.[16]

Chief Justice William Howard Taft, writing the majority opinion for the Supreme Court, accepted most of the arguments that had been made earlier by Madison and Jackson.[17] He claimed that Senate participation in

14. Even Corwin sees the need to counter the tendency to evaluate Johnson's Presidency in simply negative terms. Corwin notes that Johnson not only escaped removal but won a major victory in the case of *Mississippi v. Johnson*, 71 U.S. (4 Wall.) 475 (1867). In that case the Court refused to issue an injunction against the President, claiming it would be unable to enforce it. See Corwin, *The President*, 25.

15. When he became President, Grant called for repeal of the Tenure of Office Act, but to the disappointment of his supporters he settled for a compromise that allowed the President to remove an official only after the Senate had confirmed that official's replacement. For a discussion of Grant's failure, see Sidney Milkis and Michael Nelson, *The American Presidency: Origins and Development* (Washington, D.C.: Congressional Quarterly Press, 1990), 165–69. The Act was formally repealed in 1887.

16. In 1876 Congress had passed an act saying that all first-, second-, and third-class postmasters could be removed by the President only with the advice and consent of the Senate.

17. *Myers v. U.S.*, 272 U.S. 52 (1926). Taft spoke for the majority of a divided Court; McReynolds, Brandeis, and Holmes dissented. Holmes made the most radical legislative

removal would be an unconstitutional infringement on the legitimate sphere of executive authority and that it would rob the President of the authority necessary to carry out his constitutional responsibilities as head of the executive branch. Taft was clear that the doctrine of legislative supremacy was inconsistent with the constitutional separation of powers.

Justice Taft, however, recognized some limits on the President's powers. Congress could have legitimately restricted the removal power of the President over inferior officers, just as it had done in the creation of the Civil Service. There were limits on the President's removal power, but according to Taft, they did not apply in this case.

The reason they did not apply, Justice Taft argued, was that first-class postmasters were appointed by the President with the advice and consent of the Senate.

> Congress deemed appointment by the President with the consent of the Senate essential to the public welfare, and, until it is willing to vest their appointment in the head of the Department, they will be subject to removal by the President alone, and any legislation to the contrary must fall as in conflict with the Constitution.[18]

According to Taft, the appointment and removal power are essentially executive and may be limited only under certain specific circumstances spelled out in the Constitution. Under the Constitution, the President is empowered to appoint the heads of departments and other important executive branch officials with the advice and consent of the Senate. The President's power is limited only in regard to inferior officers, who may be appointed by the President alone, the heads of departments, or the courts. Congress may place limits on presidential removal only when it has determined "first that the officer is inferior, and second that it is willing that the office shall be filled by appointment by some other authority than the President with the consent of the Senate."[19] The *Myers* case clearly does not meet the second criterion. It is more analogous to the conditions described in *Shurtleff v. U.S.*, in which the Supreme Court concluded: "Congress has regarded the office of sufficient importance to make it proper to fill it by appointment by the President and confirmed by the Senate. It has thereby classed it as appropriately coming under the direct supervision of the President."[20]

---

supremacy argument, claiming that because Congress created the office it could place any restrictions on removal that it desired.

18. *Myers v. U.S.*, 163.

19. *Myers v. U.S.*, 162.

20. *Shurtleff v. U.S.*, 189 U.S. 311, 315, as quoted in *Myers v. U.S.*, 163.

Justice Taft, however, is willing to concede that the postmaster of Portland, Oregon, is an inferior officer. But in so doing Taft appears to create a third category of office: "important inferior office." These important inferior offices are identified by the fact that they are to be appointed by the President with the advice and consent of the Senate. But this new category of offices is not found in the Constitution.

If these offices are of "sufficient importance" to warrant presidential appointment and Senate consent, why should we not consider them superior offices? Would it not be more logical to conclude that the method of appointment was the clearest way to distinguish between superior and inferior offices under the Constitution? Offices appointed by the President with Senate consent are superior, and those appointed by other means are inferior. Rather than create this strange hybrid of "important inferior offices," it is more logical to conclude that when Congress decides that an office is of sufficient importance to warrant presidential appointment and Senate consent, it has determined that such offices are superior. It might seem odd to speak of a Portland, Oregon, postmaster as a superior executive officer, and that fact might lead Congress to reconsider its decision to use presidential appointment and Senate consent in this instance. Nonetheless, the failure of Congress to use the appropriate method of appointment in this case in no way undermines the principle that the method of appointment is the best indicator of the importance of the office.

Although Justice Taft did not suggest that the method of appointment be used as a dividing line between superior and inferior offices, he clearly accepted the principle that the Constitution associated important executive offices with presidential appointment and Senate consent. Moreover, he concluded that it was only within the sphere of inferior executive offices that limits on the President's removal power are found.

These possible qualifications on the removal power came to light more clearly in *Humphrey's Executor v. U.S.*[21] William Humphrey was a member of the Federal Trade Commission during the New Deal. Franklin Roosevelt, however, believed that Humphrey was thwarting New Deal policies and should be replaced. When Humphrey refused to offer his resignation, Roosevelt removed him from office. Humphrey died shortly after his removal, but his wife brought suit, claiming that President Roosevelt had no power to remove a member of an independent regulatory commission. Independence could be maintained only if the President was forbidden to remove commissioners for political reasons.

21. *Humphrey's Executor v. U.S.*, 295 U.S. 602 (1935).

Many thought that the opinion in the *Myers* case provided support for Roosevelt's action. If members of the executive branch were to be held politically responsible through the President's removal power, then that power must extend to all important members of the executive branch, including members of independent regulatory commissions (IRCs). After all, they were appointed by the President with the advice and consent of the Senate. But the Supreme Court decided that the IRCs were not simply part of the executive branch. They exercised "quasi-legislative and quasi-judicial functions." Moreover, the reason for their creation was to take certain areas of regulation out of the political arena. Political independence, and in some cases technical expertise, were to provide the grounds for decision. Presidential removal would inevitably lead to repoliticization.

This decision does raise some troubling questions for maintenance of the separation of powers.[22] The IRCs, by the Supreme Court's definition, do not fit neatly into the separation-of-powers framework. Because they do not, there is no clear means of establishing political responsibility.[23] The IRCs are truly the most elitist institutions in our government.

Although the constitutional status of the IRCs is ambiguous, the Court was drawing, at least indirectly, on some constitutional qualifications on the President's removal power. The IRCs do perform a quasi-judicial function, and the Constitution recognizes the need for judicial independence. Even though the President may appoint judges, he has no power of removal over them. The distinction between inferior and superior offices also comes into play. The reason the President is given less control over inferior offices is that such offices are largely involved in carrying out ministerial functions. It is only at the higher levels of administration that significant political discretion is exercised. Although in practice it is hard to argue that the IRCs do not exercise considerable political discretion, at least in theory one could claim that their decisions are based on technical expertise rather than political considerations. Technical decisions may have far-reaching political consequences, but they are more ministerial than political in character. The technician tells us how a political goal can best be achieved, but not what the political goal should be. In this sense the member of the IRC might be seen as an inferior officer, a higher level version of a civil servant. He is a technical instrument for use by the politi-

---

22. Corwin (*The President*, 90) argues that the opinions in *Myers* and *Humphrey* are in conflict with one another.

23. This was the argument the Brownlow Commission made. See President's Committee on Administrative Management, *Administrative Management in the Government of the United States* (Washington, D.C.: Government Printing Office, 1937), 36.

cal process. He can serve his function only if he maintains a certain degree of independence.[24]

The IRCs point to nonlegislative restraints on the exercise of executive power and on the President's power to control his appointees. These pools of independent discretion stand outside the executive branch in the case of judicial power, but coexist within the executive branch in the case of inferior offices. They do qualify presidential discretion. But what is even more interesting is the fact that these pools of discretion do not come under the direct power of the legislature, and may even aid the President in checking the legislature. This discretionary authority is another example of the limits of law. A government of laws cannot work without the existence of individuals wielding discretionary authority. Thus, executive branch discretion, even when beyond the immediate reach of the President, enhances executive power and restricts legislative power.

The judiciary and the IRCs only serve to amplify the point that we can never have simply a government of laws. The laws passed by the legislature provide a framework, a set of guidelines for the exercise of political authority, but both the Constitution and the laws give rise to the exercise of legitimate discretionary authority. In some cases constitutional goals may best be pursued by politically independent subordinates. If, however, that discretion is to be held politically accountable, it will be through the office of the Presidency. In no case does the legislature exercise direct political control through a power of removal.

This principle has been upheld in recent Supreme Court cases. The *Synar* case, discussed in Chapter 3, follows the principles laid down in *Myers*.[25] By denying the right of Congress to lodge the power of sequestration in the office of the Comptroller General, a legislative branch official, the Supreme Court reaffirmed the principle that executive functions must be performed by the executive branch and that executive branch officials must be under the political control of the President. And although the case of *Nixon v. Fitzgerald* dealt explicitly with the issue of the President's legal immunity, it resulted in the Court's refusal to allow the President to be sued for removing an executive branch official.[26] Even though Fitzgerald, as a whistle-blower, was acting in what he thought to be the public interest, the Court claimed that President Nixon could not be held liable for dismissing him. Fitzgerald may have been right, but Nixon was

24. This point is stressed by the Hoover Commission Report. See Commission on the Organization of the Executive Branch of Government, *Task Force Report on Regulatory Commissions* (Washington, D.C.: Government Printing Office, 1949).

25. *Bowsher v. Synar*, 478 U.S. 714 (1986).

26. *Nixon v. Fitzgerald*, 457 U.S. 731 (1982).

President, and as President he was politically but not legally accountable for his direction of the executive branch.

However, in the case of *Morrison v. Olson* the Supreme Court failed to uphold the President's removal power.[27] But before looking at that case, it will be instructive to discuss the issue of the legislative veto.

THE RISE AND FALL OF THE LEGISLATIVE VETO

With the Supreme Court's decision in *Myers*, Congress essentially lost the battle over removal. Whatever qualifications there might be on the President's removal power, neither the Senate nor the Congress as a whole would be permitted to play a direct role in removal. But Congress did not give up the possibility of exercising greater control over the executive branch. With the advent of the New Deal and President Roosevelt's broad emphasis on executive branch decision-making, Congress became even more concerned about a large bureaucracy under the control of the President. The legislative veto provided a convenient means to address the problem.

When Herbert Hoover wanted to reorganize the executive branch in 1932, he did not want to have the details of the reorganization subject to the scrutiny and revision of the normal legislative process. He wanted to be able to implement a coherent reform of the executive office. Congress was sympathetic to his plea to remodel his own office, but they did not want to establish a precedent for unilateral executive action. The compromise was that Hoover would be allowed to develop a plan, and that plan, as a whole, would take effect unless it was vetoed by Congress within sixty days. Thus, the legislative veto was born.[28]

From the 1930s through the mid-1970s the legislative veto became a popular tool of the legislature. As the President and the executive branch made more and more decisions, decisions that had the force of law or that created policy, Congress needed some mechanism by which to maintain authority. Often Congress was happy to turn over the power to make authoritative decisions to the executive branch. In some instances it did not possess the requisite knowledge or information. In others, it was simply politically more convenient to pass the buck. But to turn such

27. *Morrison v. Olson*, 487 U.S. 654 (1988).
28. *Legislative Appropriations for Fiscal Year 1933* (47 Stat. ch. 314, pp. 413–15; P. L. 72-212; approved June 1932).

extensive powers over to the executive without limitation would have greatly weakened the power of Congress. The legislative veto allowed members of Congress to believe that they were still in control. The executive was merely doing their bidding, and if he ceased to do so in a particular case the error could be quickly corrected. The President went along with the veto, considering it a minor price to pay for an expansion of executive authority.[29]

The rise of the legislative veto remained largely unnoticed until the 1970s, when a Congressman from Georgia, Elliot Levitas, introduced legislation that would make all executive branch rule-making subject to a legislative veto. Levitas claimed that the extent of executive branch rule-making was so great that Congress had in effect ceded its legislative authority to the executive branch.[30] The only way to reassert its authority would be to subject all executive branch decisions to a legislative veto. Levitas's proposal failed to pass, but the issue of the legislative veto had come to the fore. In 1983 the case of *INS v. Chadha* reached the Supreme Court, and for the first time the constitutionality of the veto was to be considered by the Court.[31]

Chadha had obtained a visa to live in the United States, but when the visa expired Chadha stayed. Under the Immigration Act, any alien remaining in the United States after the expiration of his visa was subject to immediate deportation. The Immigration and Naturalization Service initiated deportation proceedings against Chadha and determined that under the law he should be deported. But the Immigration Act allowed Chadha to appeal to the Attorney General of the United States requesting a suspension of the deportation order. Chadha did so, and the deportation order was suspended. Things were looking up for Chadha, but almost a year after the Attorney General had acted, the House of Representatives invoked the legislative veto provision of the Immigration Act that allowed either house of Congress to revoke the suspension of the deportation order within one year of the Attorney General's action. Chadha then brought suit, claiming that the suspension of the deportation order should stand because the legislative veto is unconstitutional.

Many commentators believed that Chadha's position might be upheld

29. For a discussion of the development of the veto and its constitutionality, see Murray Dry, "The Congressional Veto and the Constitutional Separation of Powers," in *The Presidency in the Constitutional Order* (Baton Rouge: Louisiana State University Press, 1981), 195–233; and Louis Fisher, *Constitutional Conflicts Between Congress and the President* (Princeton: Princeton University Press, 1985), 162–83.

30. For a discussion of the Levitas proposal, see James Sundquist, *The Decline and Resurgence of Congress* (Washington, D.C.: The Brookings Institution, 1981), 352–53.

31. *Immigration and Naturalization Service v. Chadha*, 462 U.S. 919 (1983).

on the grounds that any veto should be approved by both houses of Congress. But Chief Justice Warren Burger went further in his majority opinion. He claimed that the entire concept of the legislative veto was unconstitutional because it conflicted with the President's legitimate authority under the separation of powers. The President had won another legal victory in the struggle to control administrative discretion.

But the decision in *Chadha* is only partially consistent with the Constitution. Justice Burger reached the right decision but for the wrong reasons. Burger claimed that the problem with the veto was that it infringed on the President's *legislative* powers. Because the veto had the effect of law, Burger argued, it must be approved by the normal legislative process. This process includes not only passage by both houses of Congress, but also presentment to the President for his signature or veto. Chadha's legal status could not be changed without recourse to the legislative process, and that must include the President's role in the process.

Burger explicitly rejected Justice Byron White's dissenting argument that there is a presumption in favor of the veto merely because it has been around for forty years and has appeared in hundreds of laws. Burger explained that the veto's prevalence only heightens the need for constitutional scrutiny. The test of constitutionality is emphatically not the prevalence of the practice. Burger also rejected White's contention that because the veto provision is included in legislation passed by both houses of Congress and presented to the President, it has been legitimated by the normal legislative process. By this argument, anything the legislature did would be legitimate. The standard of constitutionality would be thrown out the window, and the doctrine of judicial restraint would have culminated in a denial of the power of judicial review.

But White also raised an important problem with Burger's reasoning. White argued that if the legislative veto is unconstitutional, so too is the power of the Attorney General to suspend the deportation order in the first place. The Attorney General is altering Chadha's legal status without going through the normal legislative process. That is, if Congress cannot change Chadha's legal status once the Attorney General suspends the deportation order, the Attorney General cannot suspend the deportation order itself. Both acts would controvert the normal legislative process. Conversely, if Burger is willing to accept the legitimacy of the delegation of authority to the Attorney General, White argued, he must also accept the legitimacy of the veto.[32]

---

32. Constitutional scholars made the same argument. Murray Dry points to the need for delegation of authority in modern government and to the legitimacy of placing conditions on that delegation. See Dry, "Congressional Veto," 201–5. Dry also cites Corwin, who asked,

White thinks that the Supreme Court must accept both the initial delegation of authority and the legislative veto. If the Court decided to reject both, he believes it would have to resurrect the nondelegation doctrine and thereby render illegitimate the entire apparatus of the administrative state. There may be a kind of logic to the notion that the legislature cannot even willingly give up its powers to another branch. And that notion did find judicial expression in *Fields v. Clark, Panama Refining v. Ryan,* and *Schecter Poultry v. U.S.*[33] But the nondelegation doctrine has not been applied since the New Deal, and to apply it today would render the government incapable of governing. It would be impossible for every authoritative rule or decision of the government to be approved by the normal legislative process. Having allowed the legislature to create the administrative state, White contended, it makes no sense to object when Congress tries to institute a means of checking its creation. But then we are left with the presumption that whatever is, is constitutional. The administrative state survives only if we destroy the underpinnings of judicial review and the constitutional separation of powers.[34]

In a concurring opinion, Justice Lewis Powell began to point us out of our difficulty. Powell claimed that the Court does not even have to get to the broad question of the constitutionality of the veto in general, because in this case the veto denies Chadha due process and constitutes a legislative infringement on judicial power. Powell explains that there is a qualitative difference between legislative and judicial power. The legislature makes general rules, whereas the judiciary applies those rules in particular cases. The legislature is institutionally suited to making general rules because it represents the entire spectrum of opinions and interests and provides a means for building consensus among those conflicting interests. The animating force behind the legislature is political, and the major check on the legislature is political.

The judiciary, on the other hand, is structured to deal with individuals. The fate of a particular individual should not be based on political pres-

---

"How is the line between delegation and abdication to be maintained? Only, I urge, by rendering the delegated powers recoverable without the consent of the delegate" (*The President*, 130).

33. *Panama Refining Company v. Ryan*, 293 U.S. 388 (1935); *Schechter Poultry Corp. v. U.S.*, 249 U.S. 495 (1935).

34. Sotirios Barber has argued that it is possible to develop a conception of the nondelegation doctrine that would provide guidance for the operation of modern American government. Barber believes that we can distinguish between delegations that are "instrumental to the exercise of power" and therefore legitimate, and delegations that are "abdications" of the exercise of power, which are illegitimate. See Sotirios A. Barber, *The Constitution and the Delegation of Congressional Power* (Chicago: University of Chicago Press, 1975), esp. 1–51.

sures. The primary justification for an independent judiciary is that it will be insulated from political pressures and allow for a fair and impartial application of the general rules passed by the legislature to individual cases. The primary check on judicial power is the principle of due process, a principle that is not operative in the legislative process. To allow Chadha's fate to be decided by the legislature is to deny him the due process of a judicial proceeding.

Justice Powell wanted to decide the case on the narrowest possible grounds. Like Justice White, he is a judicial restraintist, but unlike White he sought to preserve some constitutional basis for decision. Powell's opinion also rejected both Burger's and White's assumption that the powers involved here are legislative in nature. This assumption is consistent with White's radical restraintist perspective, but it conflicts with Burger's own desire to defend the separation of powers. Burger ignored one of the fundamental tenets of separation-of-powers theory, the idea of qualitatively different types of power. Powell sees what Burger misses: if the separation of powers is to be maintained and the integrity of the nonlegislative branches defended, one must do so by recourse to a definition of their own distinctive powers.

But Justice Powell's decision is also ultimately flawed. His restraintist's desire to make the ruling as narrow as possible prevents him from reaching the fundamental constitutional question and ultimately leaves him with an opinion that is inadequate even in this particular case. Powell never distinguishes between executive and judicial power. Given his definition of judicial power, the application of the law to individual cases, it is not clear why the power to suspend the deportation order should not also come under the heading of judicial power. If that is the case, then the Attorney General's power to suspend the order would represent an unconstitutional delegation of judicial power to the executive branch. A final determination of Chadha's legal status by the Attorney General is no more consistent with the principle of due process than the legislative veto. Like Burger, Powell never addresses the constitutionality of the delegation of authority to the Attorney General.

Justice Powell's attempt to avoid an exploration of the meaning of executive power, and the implications such an exploration would have for the general use of a legislative veto, cannot succeed. He is trapped by the same problem Justice Burger could not escape: How can you find the legislative veto to be unconstitutional without calling into question the initial delegation of authority to the Attorney General? Burger cannot explain why the initial delegation is not an unconstitutional delegation of legislative authority to the executive branch, and Powell cannot explain why it is not an unconstitutional delegation of judicial authority.

THE RIGHT REASONS

The legislative veto is unconstitutional. But to understand why, we must consider the distinctive character of executive power. Justice Powell's theory of the separation of powers has a certain plausibility. There are many similarities between executive and judicial power. Under the separation-of-powers scheme of John Locke, there was no distinction between the two.[35] Even today we can see a logic for combining them. Both are concerned with applying general rules to particular circumstances, and both point to the need for discretion in the application of the laws. But there is also a distinction. Whereas the executive is more concerned with the effective application of the laws in a given circumstance, the judiciary is more concerned with the maintenance of the principle of due process when general laws are directed against particular individuals. The *Federalist* speaks of the distinction between force and judgment.[36] More concretely, we might say that the executive wants to catch the criminal and prosecute him, whereas the judiciary is concerned that he receive a fair trial.

The reason the veto is unconstitutional in *Chadha* is that it infringes on the independent discretionary authority of the executive branch to execute the laws. In one sense the power to suspend the deportation order is akin to the President's pardoning power, a power that is not subject to the constraints of due process. Because the Attorney General will execute the decision to deport, he is given the discretion to suspend execution.

But there is also a broader concept of executive power that makes the legislative veto unconstitutional, not only in this case but in all cases. We must remember that there would be no need for an independent executive branch if the tasks to be performed were merely ministerial. It is because discretion will inevitably be exercised in the application of general laws that we need an independent political branch that can take responsibility for the use of that discretion. A multimember legislature is well suited to passing general laws, but a unitary executive is better suited to take responsibility for the discretion involved in the application of those laws.[37]

The opinions-in-writing clause provides useful guidance on this point.

35. John Locke, *Two Treatises of Government*, ed. Peter Laslett (New York: New American Library, 1965), 409–20.

36. *The Federalist*, 523.

37. Commentators such as Barber agree that the key to determining the legitimacy of the veto is an understanding of the different types of power exercised by the executive and the legislature. But, unlike me, Barber concludes that the veto may be legitimate in some cases. See Barber, *The Constitution and the Delegation of Congressional Power*, 112–17. However, our difference on this issue may not be very great, at least in practice. Barber's concept of a

As we explained in Chapter 2, the reason that the opinions of the presidential subordinates are so important is that those opinions will govern the exercise of executive discretion. There is no room for opinion in the exercise of ministerial functions; the law means what it says. But because few general laws cover every aspect of every case that will be addressed, the realm of executive power is the realm of opinion. The executive does not roam freely outside the law, but he may have a good deal of maneuvering room within the boundaries of law. The President has the constitutional right to learn the opinions of members of the executive branch, and he has the constitutional authority to remove officials when he disagrees with their opinions. He has this constitutional authority because he is the popularly elected representative and the constitutional officer responsible for the discretionary authority wielded by the executive branch.[38]

It is often a mistake to speak of Congress as delegating legislative authority to the President. What Congress in many cases does is delegate a task to the President precisely because that task is outside the competence of the legislature. This distinction has been missed by most scholars. It is almost unquestioned that when we speak of delegation we are referring to the delegation of legislative power. Why have scholars not considered the possibility that there may be a distinction between the delegation of a task and a delegation of legislative power? I think the problem is rooted in an underlying attachment to the notion of legislative supremacy. We associate definitive action with legislation. There is in this view only one fundamental type of government power—the power to make laws. Thus if we want the executive to act definitively in a particular matter, we assume that we must also want him to take over the role of the legislature. As we have seen from the various opinions in the *Chadha* case, even those like Burger who want to defend presidential power often remain trapped

---

legitimate veto is a very limited one. He argues, for example, that the veto would be legitimate in cases where the legislature has "delegated the development of viable policy proposals through periods of experimentation." Congress would in effect be deferring final action until after the results of the experimentation are known. But I would not even call this a veto. Congress is not vetoing the action of the executive. It is deferring action until it gets information from the executive. Because Congress has not acted definitively itself, there has been no delegation of authority to the executive, and the executive has taken no authoritative action that could be vetoed.

38. Commentators such as Dry show their latent legislative supremacy assumptions when they claim, "The only means of assuring a popular control over administrative rule making is to permit Congress, which is the most politically responsive branch of government, to scrutinize proposed regulations" (Dry, "Congressional Veto," 203–4). This statement ignores the extent to which the Founders created an independent popular executive precisely because they thought that such an executive would be superior to the legislature in providing popular control.

in the theory of legislative supremacy. They do not take seriously the idea of an independent and authoritative executive power that could be summoned to deal with a particular problem.

If we distinguish Congress's delegation of tasks to the executive (because those tasks are outside the competence of the legislature) from a simple delegation of legislative authority, we have a basis for declaring all legislative vetoes unconstitutional. At the same time, we recognize the legitimacy of delegating broad authority to the executive branch. If a task is given to the President in which he is to exercise discretion, Congress has implicitly defined it as an executive function—a function that must therefore be under the control of the President. Congress delegates a task to the executive because, by virtue of its unity of perspective, experience with particulars, or its access to information or technical knowledge, it is better suited to performing the task. If that is not the case, then Congress should not delegate the task. In the first instance it is Congress that makes the decision. But by delegating the task to the executive, Congress is saying that it believes the task is an essentially executive one, and thereby relinquishes its direct authority in the matter. By passing a new law, Congress can change the legal parameters in which the executive acts. It may also "influence" the executive by means of its constitutional position. But, short of legislation, it cannot require the executive to alter his use of discretion.

This theory would not only justify the existence of the administrative state, but also offer a principled and practical ground for its limitation. Some delegations might be so broad as to constitute delegation of essentially legislative functions. The Supreme Court might be more willing to declare such delegations unconstitutional if its ruling would not call the entire administrative state into question. Even the threat of judicial action would restrain Congress. More important, Congress would be more careful in its delegation of tasks if it could not reclaim the power through such mechanisms as the veto.[39] Checks would remain on the exercise of discretionary authority by the executive, but they would be political checks. The President continues to rely on Congress for appropriations. He might also fear that Congress might pass more specific laws if he uses his discretion capriciously. At the same time, responsibility for action would be more clearly established. If Congress leaves little room for executive discretion, then the law (and the Congress that passed it) will justly receive praise or blame for its success or failure. If authority is ceded by

---

39. Some studies have shown that Congress was much too optimistic in its belief that the legislative veto actually gave significant control to Congress. See, for example, Harold Bruff and Ernest Gelhorn, "Congressional Control of Administrative Regulations: A Study of Legislative Vetoes," *Harvard Law Review* 90 (May 1977), 1369–433.

the legislature to the executive, then executive responsibility will not be compromised by the existence of the legislative veto.

This type of understanding is gaining acceptance. The *Synar* case, like *Chadha,* defended executive prerogatives against legislative encroachment and actually was superior to *Chadha* in that it spoke more directly about the distinctive character of the executive branch.[40] But the Court has been uneven on this question, as can be seen in the special prosecutor case, *Morrison v. Olson.*[41] A majority opinion written by Chief Justice William Rehnquist defended the creation of a special prosecutor within the executive branch who would not be responsible to the President. The Court's conclusion rested on the assertion that the President's inability to remove the special prosecutor in no way damaged his ability to exercise his executive powers. The special prosecutor was treated as an inferior officer whose specialized function required no political control. But in so doing the Court ignored the potential for political use and abuse of the special prosecutor's powers. It denied the importance of maintaining the separation of powers and the political responsibility it helps to ensure.

Why has the Supreme Court had difficulty providing an adequate justification for the existence of independent executive authority? What has changed between *Chadha* and *Morrison* that would cause the 7–2 majority defending the President's powers in *Chadha* to become an 8–1 majority opposing the President in *Morrison?* Part of the explanation might lie in the different issues involved in the two cases, but I suspect that the shift on the part of the Court is probably primarily attributable to partisan politics.[42]

One of the most interesting and most neglected aspects of the *Chadha* case is the ideological configuration supporting and opposing the decision of the Court. Four justices wrote opinions in the case. Two, White and Rehnquist, dissented from the majority opinion of Burger, and one, Powell, wrote a concurring opinion. What is striking is that all of these justices

---

40. Nonetheless, some critics of the *Chadha* decision complain that it was not only incorrect but also ineffectual. Congress has continued to use veto-like mechanisms, and the executive has acquiesced. See Louis Fisher, "Judicial Misjudgments about the Lawmaking Process: The Legislative Veto Case," *Public Administration Review* 45 (November 1985), 705–11. But this argument misses an important point. Congress may have developed mechanisms that substitute for the legislative veto, even mechanisms that operate in ways that are in practice indistinguishable from the legislative veto, but they are not the same as a legislative veto. In fact, what is considered the ongoing use of the veto following *Chadha* is largely the kind of political accommodation that has always been encouraged by the separation-of-powers framework.

41. *Morrison v. Olson,* 487 U.S. 654 (1988).

42. One might also claim that the faulty reasoning in *Chadha* provided the basis for a complete rejection of the claims of executive power in *Morrison.*

are associated with the conservative wing of the Court. All of the members of the liberal wing, Justices William Brennan, Thurgood Marshall, Harry Blackmun, and John Paul Stevens had nothing to say, although they voted with the majority.[43] If ever there was a case where ideology would not explain the outcome, this appears to be it.

If we look not only to conservatism and liberalism but also to activism and restraint, the picture becomes clearer. We tend to associate liberalism with activism, and conservatism with restraint. An activist judiciary supports and helps to create a more liberal, activist government, whereas conservative restraintists seek to limit the expansion of government power by limiting the role the judiciary has come to play in that expansion. But it is a mistake to assume that these positions inevitably belong together.

The meanings of liberalism and conservatism are always in a state of flux. There is a tendency to assume that these labels explain more than they necessarily do, particularly when it comes to the establishment of institutional arrangements. For example, is the legislative veto a conservative or a liberal institutional device? From today's perspective the easy answer would be that it is a liberal reform. It checks the growth of the imperial Presidency, a Presidency that tends to be in the hands of Republicans and gives power to the legislature, which tends to be in the hands of the more liberal Democrats. But if that is the case, why did the liberals silently acquiesce in the Court's action in *Chadha?*

The liberal members of the Court were of a generation that associated the growth of the administrative state and the executive discretion it entailed with the growth of liberal government more broadly. The legislative veto may have appeared as just the most recent conservative attempt at reform that would restrict the expansion of government power that began in the New Deal.

It is also possible that the liberals on the Court recognized, at least on some level, that it is difficult to defend judicial discretion and independence if you do not defend executive discretion and independence. Thus, there were good reasons for the liberals to vote with the majority, but there were also good reasons for their silence. Although the liberals support an activist government, including an activist judiciary and an activist Presidency, they did not see such activism as an outgrowth of the constitutional separation of powers. To them the constitutional separation of powers is an obstacle to activist government, an obstacle that could be overcome only by an appeal to democratic values.[44]

43. The ninth Justice was Sandra Day O'Connor, who was associated with the moderate-to-conservative wing of the Court. She voted with the majority and wrote no opinion.

44. Of course, conservatives such as White are appealing to democratic values, but they use those values to justify restraint on the part of the Court, and in this case to justify congressional restraint of the executive.

The confusion for conservatives was even greater. Following Watergate, the growing Republican dominance of the executive, and the continued Democratic dominance in Congress, conservatives were becoming more favorably disposed to the Presidency. The main hope for conservatives in their battle to restrain the growth of government rested with their ability to control the office of the President, and in turn with the President's having sufficient power to control or restrain the government as a whole.

On the other hand, conservatives continued to see an activist judiciary as one of the primary means of promoting liberal policies. As long as members of the Supreme Court believed their role was to make policy rather than apply specific constitutional restrictions in specific cases, the growth of liberal government would continue. Conservatives believed that they had a chance to win the ideological war on the battleground of public opinion, the ground on which the President and Congress operated. But unless they could restrict the activities of the Court, they would ultimately be doomed to failure. The best way to restrict judicial activism was to deny power to the Court and defer to the more political branches.

The *Chadha* decision placed these two aspects of conservatism on a collision course. The conservatives, such as White and Rehnquist, who believed the primary concern was to restrict judicial activism were forced to defer to the judgment of the legislature in creating the legislative veto. Conservatives like Burger and Powell who thought it more important to check Congress than to check either the President or the Courts were willing to have the Court step in and declare the veto unconstitutional. It was a coalition of the latter strand of conservative justices with the necessarily silent liberal justices that created a majority in *Chadha*.

But as we have seen, in spite of their attempt to provide a constitutional defense of presidential power, the conservatives ultimately fail. They fail because of the pervasive influence of the doctrine of restraint on the conservative wing of the Court. Powell and Burger, who act to overturn the veto, cannot adequately justify their actions because they are trapped within the restraintist perspective. Powell does not reach the fundamental constitutional issue of the case because, in the spirit of judicial restraint, he wants to make the narrowest ruling possible. Burger, who certainly tries to defend the President, ends up doing so on the grounds of his legislative powers. Because restraintists want to defer to legislative judgments, they tend to see government strictly in terms of laws. Discretion can be an engine for unchecked growth. Thus the safest route is to deny discretionary authority, whether it be judicial or executive in character. By focusing on the President's legislative authority, Burger can avoid defending the kind of constitutional discretionary authority that might support an activist conservative President but might also support an activist liberal Court.

We need to find a Supreme Court justice who is able to defend the separation of powers based on an understanding of three distinct types of authority created by the Constitution. The liberals long ago sought to escape the limits of a constitutional framework, whereas the conservatives have become paralyzed by the fear that to admit the existence of discretionary authority within the Constitution will open the floodgates of activist government.

Morrison v. Olson helps to illustrate the dimensions of the problem. In a 7–1 decision (Antonin Scalia dissented, and Anthony Kennedy recused himself in this case) the Court upheld the creation of the special prosecutor.[45] Many conservatives were surprised by the decision. After all, since the time of *Chadha* two Reagan appointees had been added to the Court, and Rehnquist had been elevated to the office of Chief Justice. Given this ideological shift, how could one explain the Court's decision to go against the Reagan administration?

Justice Blackmun contended that the administration position was so clearly in error that only the most ideological of the justices—Scalia— would dare to defend it.[46] But even without a close examination of the opinions in the case, I believe another explanation is more plausible. First of all, the doctrine of restraint had grown in strength on the conservative wing of the Court during the Reagan years. Burger, who wrote the majority in *Chadha* and who was most willing to defend executive prerogatives, was no longer on the Court and was no longer Chief Justice. Thus the conservative restraintists were in the driver's seat and were willing to follow their restraintist doctrine to its logical conclusion. They would defer to the legislature, even if that meant going against a conservative President and defending a liberal legislature.

The conservative wing had logically evolved, given the constitutional principles its members espoused. The liberal position is more difficult to explain. It was the liberals who provided the majority in *Chadha*, albeit silently. How could the liberals defend judicial discretion and judicial activism and not defend executive prerogatives? The only possible answer is political. By the time of this case the Presidency was firmly established as the bastion of opposition to liberal activist government. Having no constitutional standard for their defense of institutions, they now turned against the executive because Reagan was the President, and the Presidency had become anathema to the policy position of the liberals.

---

45. The alignment of the Court in *Morrison* clearly paralleled that found in *Mistretta v. U.S.*, 488 U.S. 109 (1989), in which the Court upheld the creation of sentencing commissions by a vote of 8 to 1. Only Scalia dissented in this case, claiming the sentencing commissions represented an unconstitutional violation of legislative authority.

46. Justice Blackmun, who was by chance my seatmate on a flight between Washington and New York, made this comment to me.

What the liberals seem to have forgotten is that the kind of active government they desire requires the exercise of discretionary authority. The public may not be as shortsighted as they think. If the current attack of the liberals on discretionary executive authority succeeds (as well as their more recent attack on "conservative judicial activism"), they may find themselves at a great disadvantage when they hold the Presidency. They fail to appreciate this fact because they fail to appreciate the power of the Constitution in American politics. They believe that they created a powerful Presidency by means of popular leadership, completely neglecting the constitutional supports for executive power that were ultimately responsible for their success.

Conservatives, on the other hand, have failed to appreciate that discretionary authority and limited government are not irreconcilable. To the contrary, the major support for limited government is the constitutional separation of powers.[47] But that separation becomes meaningless if it is not the product of distinctive types of power. Without such distinctions the branches will collapse into one another. Conservatives fail to recognize this because they tend to emphasize the limits of government. They want a limited government of laws, rather than a government of people wielding discretionary authority. They have become too enamored of the belief that laws serve to limit whereas discretion serves to expand power. They need to learn that laws are the ultimate means of extending power and that discretion in their implementation may serve to restrain the overreaching of the legislature.[48]

The modern administrative state is not an aberration. It is a logical outgrowth of modern constitutional government. If we fail to understand

47. Terry Eastland, *Energy in the Executive: The Case for the Strong Presidency* (New York: The Free Press, 1992), 2–3, makes a similar point regarding conservative ambivalence toward executive power.

48. Only Scalia is willing to take seriously the centrality of the separation of powers to the operation of constitutional government, and only he is willing to defend an independent executive wielding discretionary authority. However, Scalia's defense of presidential authority may go too far. It is not clear from Scalia's dissents whether he would find any basis for the existence of independent regulatory commissions or even for civil service. Both would appear to unduly restrict the President's control of the executive branch in Scalia's view. But, as argued above, the Constitution appears to leave some room for executive authority not under the direct control of the President.

At least until the confirmation of Clarence Thomas, Scalia's influence among his colleagues was quite limited. Increasingly he is viewed merely as an "extreme" conservative. But it is not apparent that his view of the separation of powers can be reduced to some version of conservative ideology. To the contrary, it appears that Scalia's theory of the separation of powers is neutral in regard to the policies to be pursued. Those who see a defense of executive power as necessarily conservative have little historical sense or little appreciation of recent political changes. Indeed, it will be interesting to see what effect the Clinton Presidency will have on partisan attitudes toward the executive branch.

this, we will never be able to understand what limits can and should be placed on its growth and operation. The legislature can directly limit administrative discretion by passing specific legislation. More often, however, it will realize the desirability of discretion. It will circumscribe the sphere of executive discretion, but it will not seek to eliminate it. The ultimate threat of a funding cutoff or more specific legislation serves as its most effective, though more indirect, means of control.

The administration has independent power, and to the extent that power is politically responsible it is subject to presidential control. It is possible that subordinate officers may have discretion based on their immediate experience or technical knowledge. The extent of political responsibility for this type of discretion is open to question, but its existence points to the need for some sphere of discretionary authority at the core of government, no matter how well circumscribed. This kind of authority is not a denial of the principles of liberalism, but is necessary in order to implement those principles.

The development of executive discretion in the administration of the laws did not represent a break with the constitutional Presidency. In this respect the myth of the modern Presidency is in error. Constitutional government must inevitably be both a government of laws and a government of "men." Few would want to eliminate the institutional restraints of constitutional government and its reliance on law, but it would be equally foolish to try to eliminate the judgment and discretion that are necessary to make even a limited government effective.

CHAPTER FIVE

Foreign-Policy Making:

Constitutional Restraint and Political Necessity

Foreign-policy making gives rise to the greatest claims of discretionary power on the part of the President because it deals with other nations, which are not subject to our constitutional restraints, and it deals with issues of national survival, which tend to dwarf other concerns. According to the myth of the modern Presidency, the increased involvement of the United States in world affairs during the twentieth century has dramatically broadened the sphere for independent executive action. Presidents have been forced to wield broad discretionary authority in order to deal with the demands of political necessity in foreign affairs. The limits of the law and the Constitution could not be applied to the successful conduct of foreign policy.

But as the President's power in foreign affairs has grown, we have witnessed increasing concern that such power is a major threat to the idea of limited constitutional government. It is feared that even necessary emergency actions may give rise to dangerous precedents—precedents that may encourage the abuse of power. How much discretionary authority should the President possess, according to the Constitution? Has the discretionary authority of the President in foreign affairs dramatically increased over time? Must the President inevitably be free to escape the bounds of the Constitution in order to address the claims of political necessity? To investigate these questions, we shall look at the development of the emergency powers doctrine in the context of the war powers debate.

CONSTRAINING THE WAR POWER

The use of force, or the "war power," is the most frequently debated topic regarding the conduct of foreign policy. The President is commander-in-chief, but what does that mean?

The War Powers Act presents an excellent example of the difficulty. It attempted to define the parameters of the presidential war power and provided for: specific criteria for the legitimate use of troops; a requirement that the President report to Congress on the use of troops within forty-eight hours of their introduction into hostilities; a time limit of sixty days for the use of troops without statutory authorization or a declaration of war (although the President could take up to an additional thirty days to extricate the troops from combat), and a provision that would allow for Congress to call for the immediate withdrawal of troops at any time by means of a concurrent resolution.[1]

In spite of its ambitious goals, the act has for the most part been unsuccessful in defining or restraining executive war powers. In the first place, the definition of the appropriate circumstances for the use of force by the executive—pursuant to (1) a declaration of war, (2) specific statutory authorization by Congress, or (3) in response to an attack on the United States, its territories or possessions, or its armed forces—occurs in the purpose and policy section of the legislation. This section is typically understood as a nonbinding statement and not as an enforceable statute. In many cases it is not even printed as a part of the U.S. legal code.[2]

Second, the provision allowing Congress to direct the President to withdraw forces from hostilities by means of a concurrent resolution at any time when there is no declaration of war or specific statutory authorization was effectively nullified by the *INS v. Chadha* decision. As we have seen, the Supreme Court decreed that Congress could not act to alter an existing legal relationship without following the constitutional provisions for legislation, which include the passage of an act by both houses of Congress and presentation of such legislation to the President for his signature

1. Public Law 93-148, 87 Stat. 555 (1973).
2. Robert Scigliano explains that the decision to place these conditions for the use of force in the purpose and policy section was the result of a compromise between the House and the Senate. The Senate wanted to establish clear conditions for the use of force, but the House believed that such conditions would shackle the President. The compromise was to place the conditions in a portion of the Act that was not legally binding. See Robert Scigliano, "The War Powers Resolution and the War Powers," in *The Presidency in the Constitutional Order*, ed. Joseph M. Bessette and Jeffrey Tulis (Baton Rouge: Louisiana State University Press, 1981), 116–17. Richard Pious, (*The American Presidency* [New York: Basic Books, 1979], 404), also stresses the importance of placing these conditions in the purpose and policy section.

or veto. Because a concurrent resolution is not presented to the President, it fails to meet the constitutional requirements set forth in *Chadha*. Thus, the only means by which Congress could directly and unilaterally order the withdrawal of troops under the War Powers Act is no longer a legitimate option.[3]

Third, many of the provisions of the War Powers Act are ambiguous. What constitutes an adequate report to Congress? To whom in Congress does such a report go? Who defines imminent hostilities? Who starts the clock for the various timetables established by the Act? All these questions are open to different interpretations by Congress and the President. It is not even clear from the Act that Congress can withdraw support for the use of troops once it has given such support. The legislation requires the President to terminate the use of troops unless Congress has declared war, enacted specific authorization, or extended by law the sixty-day period, or unless the President is unable safely to remove the troops immediately, in which case he is given an additional thirty days to terminate involvement. What these provisions do not say is what happens once Congress has given statutory authorization. The Act establishes no procedure or right for Congress to rescind such authorization, other than the now-unconstitutional process for troop withdrawal.[4]

Finally, some critics have even argued that the War Powers Act actually increased rather than limited presidential authority. According to Arthur Schlesinger Jr., the Act legitimizes the right of the President alone to decide to commit troops to combat for a period of sixty to ninety days.[5] This, in Schlesinger's view, creates a legal basis for presidential discretion, in an area that had heretofore not existed. Presidents may have acted, but the legitimacy of their actions has been at best ambiguous. This ambiguity,

3. It is likely that the Court would consider a concurrent resolution to be in violation of the *Chadha* decision, and it is also entirely possible that it would refuse to hear any challenge by Congress regarding a violation of the terms of the War Powers Act. As Richard Pious has argued, the Court might well follow the example of the court of appeals in *Crockett v. Reagan*, claiming that disputes over the terms of the War Powers Act are political questions. See Richard Pious, "Presidential War Powers, the War Powers Resolution, and the Persian Gulf," in *The Constitution and the American Presidency*, ed. Martin Fausold and Alan Shank (Albany, N.Y.: SUNY Press, 1991), 202.

4. For a discussion of the practical problems with implementing the War Powers Act, see ibid., 202–5. Even Louis Henkin, a defender of congressional control over war powers, admits that the Act was poorly drawn. See Louis Henkin, *Constitutionalism, Democracy, and Foreign Affairs* (New York: Columbia University Press, 1990), 90.

5. Arthur M. Schlesinger Jr., *The Imperial Presidency* (New York: Popular Library, 1974), 456–57. Some members of Congress raised this concern as well. For a discussion of these congressional complaints, see William B. Spong Jr., "The War Powers Resolution Revisited: Historic Accomplishment or Surrender?" *William and Mary Law Review* 16 (1975), 837–41.

liberal opponents of the Act claim, served as a kind of restraint on the actions of the President. The War Powers Act removed the ambiguity and thereby made it easier for Presidents to initiate hostilities.

In practice, the War Powers Act has never been used to limit the short-term discretion of the President. The evacuation from South Vietnam, the Mayaguez incident, and the invasion of Grenada all ignored the conditions of the Act. Even the Beirut Resolution, which nodded in the direction of the Act, was followed immediately by a presidential statement denying the Act's constitutionality.

In the Beirut crisis, the key to congressional involvement was ultimately tied to congressional funding powers rather than to the War Powers Act itself. Reagan sought a compromise with Congress because he feared a congressional cutoff of funds. It has been, and continues to be, this fear of funding restrictions that forces the President to take the views of Congress into account. There was little explicit mention of the War Powers Act by either Bush or Congress during the Persian Gulf War. Bush sought congressional support and was pleased to have received it. He was more likely to be able to sustain the operation over the long run or in the face of any temporary setbacks if Congress were on record in support of his initiative. But administration officials continued to claim that such support was not necessary for Bush to act. Thus, the War Powers Act has become a dead letter. There has even been a movement for repeal of the War Powers Act. It remains on the books only because Congress does not want to admit its failure to provide a statutory limit on the President's war powers. Because Congress cannot devise another measure that would be in practice superior to the Act, its only option is to do nothing.[6] The reasons for the difficulty become obvious if we look at the history of the war powers debate.

THE ORIGINS OF THE WAR POWERS DEBATE

The problem of defining the spheres of presidential and congressional war powers is as old as the Republic. The debate between the President and Congress goes back at least to the controversy surrounding George Wash-

---

6. In 1988 Senators Byrd, Mitchell, Warner, and Nunn introduced legislation to make major changes in the War Powers Act. In his statement announcing the proposed legislation, Nunn began by saying: "The War Powers Resolution is 'broke' and should be fixed" (Sam Nunn, "Summary Statement: War Powers Act," press release, May 19, 1988). In spite of support by some of the most powerful members of the Senate, the proposed changes were never adopted.

ington's proclamation of neutrality in 1793. Washington's proclamation was seen by the Jeffersonians as the adoption of a pro-British position and was greeted with great hostility by the Jeffersonian members of Congress. The debate not only focused on the policy of neutrality but also extended to the question of the President's right to issue a proclamation of neutrality. Alexander Hamilton, writing under the pseudonym of Pacificus, wrote a series of letters defending Washington's action, while James Madison, writing under the pseudonym of Helvidius, argued against Washington and for legislative domination in foreign policy.[7]

Hamilton's defense of Washington took a number of forms. As we noted in Chapter 1, the most persuasive case made by Hamilton was the claim that Washington acted only to state the existing policy. Hamilton claimed that in the absence of a declaration of war the United States was at peace with both sides and should therefore act accordingly. Washington, in this view, was not establishing a policy so much as giving voice to the existing state of affairs. Congress could of course declare war against Britain or France, or take other measures short of war, but in the absence of such actions Washington was free to articulate the existing policy.

Hamilton, however, did not allow his argument to rest on this point. He went on to claim that it is the President, not the legislature, who is responsible for the conduct of foreign policy. The President is

> the organ of intercourse between the nation and foreign nations— as the interpreter of the national treaties . . . —as that power which is charged with the execution of the laws, of which treaties form a part—as that power which is charged with the command and application of the public force.[8]

Hamilton explained that whereas the grant of legislative powers (All legislative powers herein granted . . .) is a limited grant, the grant of executive power (The executive power shall be vested in a President . . .) has no such limitations. It is limited only by the specific exceptions provided for in the Constitution. For example,

> the participation of the Senate in the making of treaties and the power of the Legislature to declare war are exceptions out of the

---

7. Alexander Hamilton, "The Pacificus Letters, I–VII," in *The Papers of Alexander Hamilton*, ed. Harold C. Syrett, 20 vols. (New York: Columbia University Press, 1969), 15:33–43, 56–63, 65–69, 82–86, 90–95, 100–106, 130–35; James Madison, "Helvidius Letters, 1–5," in *The Papers of James Madison*, ed. Thomas A. Mason et al. (Charlottesville: University Press of Virginia, 1985), 15:66–74, 80–87, 95–103, 106–10, 113–20.

8. Hamilton, "Pacificus, No. 1," 38.

general "Executive power" vested in the President. They are to be construed strictly—and ought to extend no further than is essential to their execution.[9]

Hamilton recognized that even under the strictest construction the foreign-policy powers of Congress were substantial, but he concluded that this in no way compromised the President's substantial powers. The powers of Congress and the President, he argued, should be understood as concurrent powers:

> The Legislature is free to perform its own duties according to its own sense of them—though the Executive in the exercise of its constitutional powers may establish an antecedent state of things that ought to weigh in the legislative decisions.[10]

The powers of each branch are legitimate, and each may operate in any given case. The legitimate actions of one branch may limit the options of the other branch, but that possibility in no way contradicts either branch's claim to authority. According to Hamilton, there is no "war power," but instead a number of powers that relate to the conduct of war and foreign policy. Some of those powers are wielded primarily by the executive and some by the legislature. The Constitution, in Hamilton's formulation, does not determine which branch will predominate in any given situation, but it provides guidelines for the operation of different kinds of power in any circumstance.

According to Madison, however, the relationship of the executive to the legislature is one of subordinate to superior:

> The natural province of the executive magistrate is to execute the laws, as that of the legislature is to make laws. All his acts, therefore, properly executive, must presuppose the existence of the laws to be executed.[11]

The executive is to act only in accordance with the laws laid down by the legislature. The executive is merely a useful tool of the legislature:

> Although the executive may be a convenient organ of preliminary communications with foreign governments, on the subjects of treaty or war; and the proper agent for carrying into execution the

9. Ibid., 42.
10. Ibid.
11. Madison, "Helvidius, No. 1," 69.

final determinations of the competent authority; yet it can have no pretensions, from the nature of the powers in question compared with the nature of its executive trust, to that essential agency which gives validity to such determinations.[12]

The executive is dependent on the legislature to provide legitimacy for its actions; it has no independent basis for legitimate action.

Madison goes on to point out the essentially legislative character of declaring war and making treaties. He argues that whereas presidential appointments require the approval of only a majority of the Senate, treaties require the approval of two-thirds of the Senate. He argues that this supermajority is a "compensation for the other branch of the legislature, which, on certain occasions, could not be conveniently a party to the transaction." Moreover treaties are to "have the force and operation of laws." They are "the supreme law of the land."[13] As such, they are clearly in the province of the legislature, according to Madison.

The case for declaring war is equally clear in Madison's mind: "Those who conduct a war cannot in the nature of things be proper or safe judges, whether a war ought to be commenced, continued or concluded."[14] The power to declare war must be separated from the power to conduct war. Those who see the power to declare war or make treaties as executive powers are at odds with fundamental principles of the Constitution and the separation of powers. They confuse the American Constitution with the British system: "The power of making treaties and the power of declaring war, are royal prerogatives in the British government, and are accordingly treated as executive prerogatives by British commentators."[15]

Those who would place such powers in the hands of the American President would prefer monarchy to the American Constitution. But Madison obviously recognized an exception to this principle. At the Constitutional Convention, it was he and Elbridge Gerry who proposed substituting the words "declare war" for the words "make war" in order to allow room for the President to use troops in response to an attack. In this instance the President would have the right to act independently of the legislature.[16]

12. Ibid.
13. Ibid., 71.
14. Ibid.
15. Ibid., 72.
16. *The Records of the Federal Convention of 1787,* ed. Max Farrand, 4 vols. (New Haven: Yale University Press, 1966), 2:318. In addition, at the end of "Helvidius, No. 1" Madison quotes favorably Hamilton's statement that "the execution of the laws and the employment of the common strength, either for this purpose, or for common defense, seem to comprise all the functions of the executive magistrate" (73). This statement also suggests that the executive may act "for the common defense" without the sanction of law.

Madison did not want to deny the President the authority to do what was necessary to protect the nation in the event of an attack, but it was only in such an emergency that Madison would allow for the executive to act on its own authority.

Even this concession to potential emergencies points to a serious problem with Madison's argument. He claimed that under the Constitution the only legitimate source of the authority for the President comes from acts passed by the legislature. But in an emergency the Congress does not have time to legislate. Thus, Madison admits that he is creating a Constitution that does not apply in all cases. Emergencies may render the Constitution irrelevant, because in emergencies the President must act independently. The Constitution under Madison's formulation does not encompass the power of self-defense.

One does not even have to go to the extreme case to see the difficulties with Madison's approach. Madison is in error on at least two other points. First, his analysis of the treaty-making power is not consistent with the arguments made at the Constitutional Convention. Whether or not some delegates saw treaty-making as essentially legislative, the primary reason for the two-thirds requirement for treaty ratification was the fear of the small states that their interests would be ignored by the President. The two-thirds requirement was included as a kind of veto mechanism, to prevent majority tyranny from injuring the small states.[17]

Second, and more fundamental, Madison's argument for legislative supremacy does not hold up in light of the debates at the Constitutional Convention. Madison's claim of legislative supremacy is closer to the view of Roger Sherman, a view decisively rejected by the Convention, than it is to the arguments made by the most influential delegates to the Convention, including himself. As we saw in Chapter 2, the Convention sought to encourage executive independence, not executive dependence.

This does not imply that executive power was to be without checks. What it does mean is that the Constitution explicitly created the executive as a co-equal branch of government with its own sources of legitimacy. The power of the Presidency comes not from the legislature, as Madison implies, but from the constitutional office and independent popular election. The Madison of the "Helvidius Letters" confuses the legislature with a Constitutional Convention. He fails to recognize that under a written Constitution the power of the President comes from the fundamental written law of the Constitution and not from the ordinary acts of the

17. See Charles Thach, *The Creation of the American Presidency, 1775–1789* (Baltimore: Johns Hopkins University Press, 1969), 164.

legislature. Both the executive and the legislature are limited because they each are dependent on the Constitution for their authority.

It is therefore appropriate that Madison, and not Hamilton, is the vehicle by which Locke's doctrine of prerogative power enters the American political tradition.[18] As we shall see in the next chapter, it is Locke, the defender of legislative supremacy, who must create an extraordinary extralegal power to defend his government. Where there is no written Constitution, there is no room within a legal framework of government for discretionary authority capable of self-defense. That is why it is Hamilton, the defender of concurrent powers, and not Madison, the defender of legislative supremacy, who finds room for discretionary authority within the context of the Constitution.[19]

THE EVOLUTION OF THE EMERGENCY POWERS DOCTRINE

On the issue of emergency powers, Americans have overestimated their debt to Locke. We have failed to appreciate the advance made by our Constitutional Convention over Lockean political theory. The separation of powers is fully realized only when each branch of government is limited by and derives its legitimacy from a written Constitution. Furthermore, the modern executive can become the equal of the legislature only when its legitimacy is grounded in popular election. Hamilton's theory of executive power shows an appreciation for these contributions of American constitutionalism, whereas Madison's theory ironically fails to appreciate the scope of the achievement of the Constitutional Convention.

18. Gary Schmitt develops a similar theory regarding the connection between Jefferson's principled defense of limited constitutional powers for the President and Jefferson's acceptance of the prerogative powers doctrine. Schmitt provides the clearest statement to date of the connection between these two theories in the thought of the founding generation. See Gary J. Schmitt, "Thomas Jefferson and the Presidency," in *Inventing the American Presidency,* ed. Thomas E. Cronin (Lawrence: University Press of Kansas, 1989), 326–46. Schmitt sees what so many others have missed, that the Whig view of government and the prerogative powers doctrine are not radically different alternatives but are fundamentally linked to one another.

19. Madison explicitly rejected the doctrine of concurrent powers, complaining that it was illogical to give the same power to two different branches at the same time ("Helvidius, No. 2," 81–84). But Madison missed a crucial element of Hamilton's argument. While Madison spoke of power, Hamilton spoke of powers. Hamilton argued that different types of power might be relevant in a given situation and that each branch could act through its own distinctive powers, not by exercising the same power at the same time.

While we have tolerated the kind of political practice supported by Hamilton, we have relied on Madison's theory to justify it. From the Barbary Pirates, through the Mexican War, the Civil War, the Spanish-American War, Korea, Vietnam, and numerous smaller incidents in between, Presidents have exercised a great deal of discretion in the use of troops. Complaints have been raised by Congress over the exercise of such discretion, but on the whole no serious constraints have been placed on the President. The exercise of presidential discretion has been reluctantly accepted.

The basis for that acceptance, however, has not been the constitutional arguments of Hamilton, but instead the escape clause in Madison's argument. For most of our history we have accepted the Lockean principles of legislative supremacy and prerogative power. Extralegal discretion has been seen as a necessary exception to the rule of law. Thomas Jefferson's argument is typical:

> A strict observance of the written laws is doubtless one of the high duties of a good citizen, but it is not the highest. The laws of necessity, of self-preservation, of saving our country when in danger are of a higher obligation. To lose our country by a scrupulous adherence to the written law, would be to lose the law itself, with life, liberty, property and all those who are enjoying them with us; thus absurdly sacrificing the end to the means.[20]

The power to repel attacks, conceded by Madison, was thereby expanded to a more general prerogative power to deal with emergencies, or to deal with the extraordinary circumstances that cannot easily be handled by the law or the legislature. Of course, by its very nature foreign policy frequently gives rise to such "extraordinary" cases.

Thus, policy-making is thought to occur on two levels: the ordinary level prescribed by the Constitution, which calls for legislative supremacy, and the extraordinary level, which allows the executive to escape from the limits of the Constitution in order to deal with extraordinary circumstances. The problem with such a system is obvious: How does one distinguish between ordinary and extraordinary circumstances? In spite of this difficulty, much of the interpretation of the war power by the Supreme Court rests on such a distinction.

Ex parte Milligan, which arose during the Civil War, begins the Supreme

---

20. Thomas Jefferson to John V. Colvin, September 10, 1810, quoted in Christopher H. Pyle and Richard M. Pious, *The President, Congress, and the Constitution* (New York: The Free Press, 1984), 63–64.

Court's development of this line of argument.[21] Lambdin Milligan was arrested by the general in charge of the military district of Indiana during the Civil War. He was convicted by a military tribunal of conspiracy to organize an insurrection behind Union lines. Milligan sought a writ of habeas corpus, charging that he had been denied his constitutional right to a trial by a civilian jury. In an apparent victory for the rule of law over the arbitrary discretion of the executive branch, the Court ruled that Milligan had the right to a civilian trial, because the civilian courts were operating in Indiana.

The opinion of the Court written by Justice David Davis was a complicated one, and it was supplemented by a qualified concurring opinion written by Chief Justice Salmon Chase. What is most interesting about the case, however, is the timing of the decision. Although Milligan was convicted during the height of the Civil War, his case was not decided by the Supreme Court until 1866. The opinion of the Court itself made reference to this delay in the following passage:

> During the late wicked Rebellion, the temper of the times did not allow that calmness of deliberation and discussion so necessary to a correct conclusion of a purely judicial question. The considerations of safety were mingled with the exercise of power; and feelings and interests prevailed which are happily terminated. Now that the public safety is assured, this question, as well as others, can be discussed and decided without passion or the admixture of any element not required to form a legal judgment.[22]

The Court admitted that it would have been unlikely to question the plea of military necessity during the crisis of the Civil War, but now that the crisis was resolved it was willing to say that actions taken during the war were inconsistent with the principles set forth in the Constitution. The use of executive power in question was clearly declared unconstitutional, but it was also recognized that neither the courts nor the Constitution would have much influence in time of war.

Thus, the Court elaborated the doctrine of emergency necessity. The rule of law provides strict limits for the use of executive power, *but* in cases of emergency the rule of law temporarily gives way to the rule of necessity. The argument in *Milligan* surely goes beyond the argument made by Madison. The emergency power referred to by Madison extended only to the immediate defense of the nation in the face of an attack. In the *Milligan*

21. *Ex parte Milligan*, 71 U.S. (4 Wall.) 2 (1866).
22. Ibid.

case, both Congress and the courts were available to make a determination. The Court did eventually rule against the executive, but in delaying its decision it sent an ambiguous message. It found the actions of the executive to be outside the Constitution, but at the same time it indicated that it would look the other way while the executive slipped out of its constitutional home in order to protect the property from an ensuing storm. The question it did not answer was: How are you going to keep the President within the Constitution once he is allowed to enjoy extraconstitutional authority?

It is this idea of extraconstitutional authority that gave rise to the most far-reaching judicial defense of executive power in foreign affairs in the case of *U.S. v. Curtiss-Wright Export Corporation*.[23] In the 1930s a threat of war existed between Bolivia and Paraguay. Congress, wanting to encourage peace, passed a resolution giving the President the power to suspend arms sales if he determined that such a suspension might promote peace. When conflict erupted, Franklin Roosevelt ordered the suspension of arms sales to both combatants. The Curtiss-Wright Export Corporation ignored the ban and was prosecuted and convicted. It appealed the conviction, claiming that the Congress had unconstitutionally delegated legislative authority to the President.

The Supreme Court claimed that the *Curtiss-Wright* case involved the conduct of foreign policy and not the delegation of ordinary legislative power. According to the Court, the power to conduct foreign policy is not subject to the same constitutional constraints as ordinary law-making. In making this distinction, the Court followed the argument developed in *Missouri v. Holland*.[24] That case involved a treaty between the United States and Canada protecting certain species of migratory birds. Missouri believed that the treaty infringed on its police powers by restricting its ability to establish hunting regulations. The state brought suit, arguing that the treaty violated the constitutional protection of federalism.

The Court responded by defending the power of the national government to make treaties. Rather than refer to the supremacy clause, however, the Court argued that the sphere of international relations stood outside the Constitution and was therefore not subject to its limitations. The power to conduct foreign affairs, the Court contended, preceded the Constitution and is an inherent power of any nation as nation. The Constitution can in no way diminish or deny that right.

In *Curtiss-Wright* the Court accepted the logic of *Missouri v. Holland* and further claimed that this extraconstitutional power to conduct foreign

---

23. *U.S. v. Curtiss-Wright Export Corp.*, 299 U.S. 304 (1936).
24. *Missouri v. Holland*, 252 U.S. 346 (1920).

policy belonged to the President. Although Justice George Sutherland defended the assignment of this power to the President in terms of his constitutional office, he nonetheless described the power as emanating from outside the Constitution. In so doing, he allowed the President to tap into a potential unlimited reservoir of power. The Court placed itself on the side of extensive extraconstitutional power for the President.

Although there have been legislative and judicial attempts to apply principled restraints on executive power, these attempts have been largely unsuccessful. We have already discussed the War Powers Act growing out of Vietnam conflict. During the Korean War, the Court denied Truman's claim of emergency powers in his takeover of the steel mills. But the question of foreign policy in the steel seizure case was confused by the fact that Truman's actions were largely directed at domestic policy concerns.[25] Direct legal or constitutional restraints have been generally unsuccessful.[26]

The more dominant principle of restraint began to emerge in a dissenting opinion in the case of *Korematsu v. U.S.*[27] Although this case has received the most attention for its defense of a racial exclusion policy directed against Japanese-Americans on the West Coast during World War II, it also raises a number of important questions involving executive power. At least in hindsight, it is obvious that racial prejudice played a major role in the army's initial exclusion orders, and the Court's ruling did not pay sufficient attention to that fact. Moreover, the majority opinion of the Court followed in the tradition of defending broad emergency powers for the President. But, for our present purposes, what is most interesting about the case is Justice Robert Jackson's dissenting opinion.

Jackson dissented because he believed that any racial classification was inconsistent with constitutional guarantees of equal protection. To allow such racial classifications under the Constitution, even if seemingly re-

---

25. *Youngstown Sheet & Tube Co. v. Sawyer*, 343 U.S. 579 (1952). Truman's decision to take over the steel mills was inextricably connected to his desire to protect the interests of labor while averting a strike.

26. Even though legal restraints have been of limited utility, scholars such as Louis Henkin still turn to them as the primary source of restraint on the President. Henkin argues: "Congress can enact laws and develop institutions so as to reaffirm our ancestral commitment to constitutionalism" (*Constitutionalism, Democracy, and Foreign Affairs*, 109). But the approach has proven to be impractical, as well as inconsistent with the theory of the separation of powers that animates the Constitution. Henkin claims that the President may act if Congress remains silent but that when Congress chooses to assert its authority the President must acquiesce. The President has no powers that are exclusive of Congress and not subject to its control. For Henkin a defense of "constitutionalism" and an assertion of legislative supremacy are synonymous (31–34). But Henkin fails to take seriously the idea of an independent executive. In our system it is the Constitution, not Congress, that is supreme.

27. *Korematsu v. U.S.*, 323 U.S. 214 (1944).

quired by an emergency, would set a dangerous precedent that would undermine constitutional support for individual liberty. But Jackson went on to say that, although unconstitutional, the action may have been necessary. In time of war, he argued, the primary consideration is one of necessity, not constitutionality. We cannot afford to concern ourselves with constitutional rights when the very existence of the nation is at stake. The emergency situation thus gives rise to extraconstitutional authority.

We are protected from an abuse of power, Justice Jackson held, because these emergency actions will not have the sanction of the Constitution or the law. By withholding constitutional sanction, Jackson hoped to keep the executive on a short leash. Even necessary actions will be repudiated after the fact. The power will evaporate once the emergency has passed; the need must be established with each case. No legal precedent will exist to create a permanent and ever-growing reservoir of power. To the contrary, the legal precedents will create a presumption against the use of such power.

Although not always explicitly stated, it is Justice Jackson's opinion that often guides the debate over emergency powers. A prime example can be found at the conclusion of the Vietnam War. On July 1, 1973, Congress adopted an amendment that denied the President funding for any further combat activities in Southeast Asia. The intention of Congress was clearly to eliminate any and all executive discretion in the use of troops in Southeast Asia. But by April 1975 the impracticality of the legislation became obvious.

The fall of South Vietnam and Cambodia was imminent, and President Gerald Ford wanted to use U.S. troops to aid in the evacuation of U.S. nationals and refugees. On April 10 he asked Congress to "clarify the 1975 restrictions." Congress did not act immediately, and two days later, with the Khmer Rouge on the outskirts of Phnom Penh, Ford directed the military to proceed with the evacuation of Cambodia—in apparent violation of congressional statute. On April 29, 1975, still awaiting congressional action, Ford ordered the evacuation of Saigon. Four soldiers were killed in the operation, and later the same day South Vietnam surrendered.[28]

Congress refused to sanction Ford's actions, even after the fact, although virtually no one thought they were inappropriate. The logic behind Congress's decision was that by refusing to authorize Ford's actions it would

---

28. For an account of this incident, see Louis Fisher, *The Constitution Between Friends: Congress, the President, and the Law* (New York: St. Martin's Press, 1978), 230–31; and Pious and Pyle, *The President, the Congress, and the Constitution*, 367–68.

discourage Ford from using the rescue operation as a justification for more extensive military operation. One wonders what Congress would have said had Ford failed to act to protect American lives. Ford was able to act only because his view of presidential authority was different from that implied in the legislation passed by Congress. He assumed that his office allowed him discretion to act without congressional authorization, even in opposition to existing legislation. But Congress, like Justice Jackson, wanted to have it both ways. They wanted the President to act, but they did not want to legitimate such extraordinary action.

RECONCILING EMERGENCY POWERS AND CONSTITUTIONAL GOVERNMENT

Justice Felix Frankfurter's concurring opinion in the *Korematsu* case offers an alternative understanding of emergency powers and the Constitution. He finds Justice Jackson's opinion to be inconsistent with the idea of limited constitutional government. Although Frankfurter understands that Jackson is attempting to restrain emergency power while allowing for its necessary exercise, he believes that Jackson's approach is unsatisfactory on both counts. First, by denying the legitimacy of emergency powers, one might cause a President to think twice at precisely the time he needs to act. There is even the danger that a well-meaning President might take seriously the idea that principles should guide action, and follow Jackson's principles to the destruction of the nation.

More likely is the other alternative, that the Constitution increasingly is seen as irrelevant to practical politics. In theory it may be pleasing, but when it is time to make important decisions we must push aside the niceties of constitutional theory for the realities of political necessity. Justice Jackson's Constitution is a Constitution that invites contempt because it is a Constitution that cannot defend itself in adversity.

Frankfurter claimed, however, that the Founders were hardheaded politicians whose theories reflected their political experience, including the experience of war. Consequently, the Constitution is a complex document that manifests itself in different ways in different circumstances. One must understand the need to emphasize different powers in different circumstances. A concern with individual rights may have to be tempered by a concern with national defense when national security is threatened. As Lincoln had said earlier, just because a particular medicine is not good for a well man does not mean it is inappropriate for one who is sick.[29] Political necessity may shift the balance of power within the Constitution.

Frankfurter emphasized this last phrase—within the Constitution. The exercise of emergency power is not uncontrollable. The judgment of circumstances must be made, as must a judgment of the effect of the use of emergency powers on the integrity of other constitutional provisions. The Court's judgment may have been incorrect in the case of *Korematsu,* but Frankfurter's argument keeps open the possibility that a judgment will be made. He wanted to provide sufficient room for discretion within the constitutional framework. Because Presidents are not forced outside that framework to effectively deal with emergencies, the Constitution can still serve a restraining function.

DEFINING PRESIDENTIAL DISCRETION

What is the character of the President's discretion in relation to the war power? The best way to understand this discretion is through an elaboration of Hamilton's concept of concurrent powers. The President directs the use of the armed forces once they are called into the service of the nation. It is easier to define the limits of this authority if there are no standing armies, or if we are faced with a total declared war. But these conditions are the exceptions and not the rule. We most often find ourselves in the middle ground, where armed forces exist under the command of the President but there is no declared war.

The President has always needed the authority to respond to attacks. He has always been faced with the potential possibility or desirability of limited actions. For most of our history he has had a standing army over which he has exercised direct command. He has been free to initiate virtually any action. He has exercised these powers because the standing army is necessary to respond to unforeseen circumstances and because the standing army must have a unified command structure.

How is this discretion restrained? The legal restraints are the least important. The power to declare war is applicable in only a limited number of circumstances. It is not suited to limited wars—certainly in the twentieth century but also in earlier years of the Republic. Even when a declaration is issued, it is more of an aid to presidential power than a restraint.

29. "Letter to Erastus Corning and Others, June 12, 1863," in *The Collected Works of Abraham Lincoln,* ed. Roy Basler, 8 vols. (New Brunswick, N.J.: Rutgers University Press, 1953), 6:267.

The declaration provides a statement of congressional support that is not easily rescinded.

The power of the purse is actually the most important congressional power in foreign policy. Congress must raise and support an army or navy before a President can command it. One might even imagine a more legitimate and more workable version of the War Powers Act, if the Act was tied directly to the funding power of Congress. If the current Act was seen merely as a preliminary step in a decision to cut funding, rather than an attempt by Congress to control executive discretion, it might have a sounder constitutional foundation. By creating a step prior to a cutoff, Congress may encourage the President to stop and listen to its concerns without intruding into the legitimate sphere of executive authority. Any cutoff of funds that did occur would be more publicly defensible if the President is given a chance to compromise.[30] Unfortunately, this is not how the Act was conceived or how it has been used.[31]

Reformers have refused to recognize that the most important restraints on executive power are political, not legal. Long-term actions require long-term financial support from Congress. If short-term actions are at odds with Congress or public opinion, they may undermine overall policy goals. At some point in the future, the President will need public and congressional support. Because Presidents recognize these political realities, the threat of tyranny or the arbitrary exercise of power is remote.

This analysis is not anticongressional. All governments need the qualities possessed by a unified and independent executive. Congress is not institutionally suited to a more direct role in the war power. It is too numerous, and it represents the diversity of interests rather than a unified

30. Louis Fisher made a similar suggestion in 1978. He claimed that linking the War Powers Act to the appropriations power would allow Congress to operate "from a solid base of constitutional authority" (*Constitution Between Friends*, 245).

31. Robert Scigliano also offers an interesting defense of the War Powers Act. He claims that the Act does not and cannot claim to restrict the use of emergency powers, which are by their definition extraconstitutional. It does not "limit the president's ability to act . . . [but it provides] means whereby Congress could judge the propriety of his actions" (Scigliano, "War Powers Resolution," 145–46). But Scigliano's defense rests on acceptance of the notion that prerogative powers are not only extralegal, but also extraconstitutional. He does not believe that emergency powers can find a place within the Constitution. Scigliano reads the Constitution as if it were synonymous with Lockean principles. But Locke did not provide for a Constitution that would be superior to the ordinary acts of the legislature, so in Locke's theory there is no basis for the distinction between extralegal (in the sense of actions not sanctioned by the legislature) and extraconstitutional authority. A written Constitution makes possible such a distinction. Scigliano himself admits (142) that the Constitution at the least acknowledges the need for some type of emergency power, and that acknowledgment suggests that the Constitution may encompass what ordinary laws may not: executive discretion to deal with emergencies.

perspective. If Congress tries to take a more direct role in foreign-policy decision-making, it may even find that the attempt backfires.

If Congress is forced to reach a definitive judgment before any limited action may be taken, it may be more rather than less likely to jump on a presidential bandwagon. Lyndon Johnson could have gotten a declaration of war or anything else he wanted in 1966. If Congress tries to imitate the President, it may cease to represent the diversity of interests in the nation, and thereby lose the perspective from which to check the executive's foreign-policy decisions.

Congress works best when it raises questions about parts of the President's policies and when it questions the effects of policy on particular interests. It should reject presidential initiatives completely only when rejection is the product of a consensus on the part of Congress and the public. And it should act indirectly through its constitutional powers of the purse rather than directly through a usurpation of executive authority.

Presidents do have the power to perform short-term actions, with public opinion being the major check. The President cannot undertake long-term use of force without congressional and public support. There is a presumption in favor of presidential initiatives, but those initiatives must ultimately rest on a political consensus in favor of presidential authority.

The presumption of authority in favor of one branch encourages action. The possibility of a check encourages the President to take into account concerns of Congress in formulating initiatives. If Congress places so many constraints on presidential action that he is unable to act, then Congress will be held accountable for the policy. If the President ignores an important interest or constituency, Congress will initiate a check. Although the separation of powers is often seen as supporting a tendency toward inaction, it actually ensures that action will be defensible and effective. To take initiative away from the President, Congress must take dramatic action and clearly assume responsibility for its decision.

The arguments against presidential discretion are not persuasive. There is no constitutional alternative to such discretion. The only alternative is the extraconstitutional authority proposed by Madison, but that alternative is unacceptable. It not only delegitimizes the necessary exercise of executive power, but also ultimately relinquishes any ability to constrain executive power. Under our written Constitution, the President's sphere of authority is constrained by Congress and public opinion, but within that sphere the President exercises independent authority. Congress may dominate in some cases—but the system should be seen not as an invitation to struggle but as an invitation to consensual action.

The genius of the Constitution is that it both constrains discretion and creates pools of discretion, and encourages the exercise of discretion within those spheres. The myth of the modern Presidency fails to recognize the possibility that these pools of discretion might exist within the Constitution. But this should not come as a surprise. Foreign policy is only the most dramatic example of the complex relationship between effective government and constitutional restraints. As we shall see in the next chapter, the problem of reconciling the demands of political necessity with the desire for legal constraints is at the core of liberal political theory.

CHAPTER SIX

The Theoretical Origins of the Modern Liberal Executive

The myth of the modern Presidency ultimately reflects a deeper problem in our understanding of the character of liberal government. Our popular conceptions of liberal political theory leave us dissatisfied with and distrustful of our political practice. This dichotomy between theory and practice is the source of some of the most serious problems for our political system.[1]

As we have seen, our understanding of liberal political theory often leads us to distrust executive power as a threat to the rule of law. The effective exercise of executive power or influence is seen as a usurpation of legislative prerogatives. Thus Presidents must often exaggerate the emergency character of situations in order to justify a departure from the strict rule of law, or they must offer convoluted legal justifications for actions that are and should be essentially discretionary. They are forced to distort their actions in order to conform to an unrealistic and theoretically indefensible set of principles.

These inadequate ideals are a threat not only to the effective exercise of executive power but also to effective constitutional restraints. Inevitably discretionary authority will be exercised. If the exercise of such authority cannot be comprehended by our principles, then our principles will ulti-

---

1. Samuel Huntington makes a similar point about the conflict between theory and practice in American politics. He notes that Americans fail to reconcile their ideas of legitimacy with their desire for effective political action. Samuel P. Huntington, *American Politics: The Promise of Disharmony* (Cambridge, Mass.: Harvard University Press, 1981).

mately be powerless to restrain it. Our theory and practice are at war with each other. We seek effective government in practice, but we want to deny the legitimacy of the authority necessary for effective government. Because our theory does not address the realities of practical politics, it can never be a guide to or a constraint on practice.

This division between theory and practice is neither inevitable nor necessary. The split is based on an inadequate understanding of the theory of modern liberal government in general and the constitutional foundations of the American Presidency in particular. The liberal tradition has been misunderstood and misrepresented. Executive power is not the traditional enemy of liberal government.[2] Tensions do exist between the idea of exec-

2. My analysis of the relationship between liberal government and executive power owes much to the work of Harvey C. Mansfield Jr. Mansfield's "Ambivalence of Executive Power," in *The Presidency in the Constitutional Order*, ed. Joseph M. Bessette and Jeffrey Tulis (Baton Rouge: Louisiana State University Press, 1981), 314–33, provided the foundation for the ideas presented in this chapter. Most of the work on this chapter had been completed before Mansfield's *Taming the Prince: The Ambivalence of Modern Executive Power* (New York: The Free Press, 1989) was published. After reading Mansfield's book, I considered eliminating this chapter altogether, but I have included it for several reasons. My argument is more limited in scope than Mansfield's; I have not attempted to do an exhaustive study of the development of executive power. I am attempting to show how the contemporary understanding or misunderstanding of the relationship between liberal government and executive power bears on our understanding of the constitutional Presidency. Thus, this chapter provides a necessary step in my argument. Second, my presentation of the material differs considerably from Mansfield's. While his book weaves together a complex theory of executive power, I have tried to separate a few of the strands of the modern theory of executive power in order to isolate the origins of some contemporary political perspectives. Finally, my analysis of the development of executive power may be more optimistic than Mansfield's. Mansfield is ultimately "ambivalent" about the taming of the prince. He rightly fears that in the process of taming the prince we may have lost an appreciation for some of the harsher but still necessary aspects of executive power. It is to a recovery of these necessary elements of executive power that Mansfield's work is directed. He does not deny that the development of the idea of executive power has in some respects represented an advance in political theory and political practice, but his emphasis on what has been lost in that process may lead to a greater pessimism toward the future of liberal government and the modern executive than is appropriate. The Framers of the American Constitution, and the early modern political philosophers who provide the theoretical underpinnings of their work, constantly remind us of the dangers and shortcomings of democracy. Democracy, like all forms of government, has its own dangerous propensities, and if we ignore those propensities we will doom democracy to failure. But if we become preoccupied with these dangers we may forget the basis of our commitment to democracy in the first place. While the democratization of the modern executive has resulted in a restraint of executive power, it also provides a new source of energy for the executive. Mansfield is correct in reminding us that this new source of energy is not without its dangers and that excessive restraint of executive power may render it incapable of performing its proper function. We should recognize, however, not only the potential conflict at the core of the theory of the modern executive but also the potential benefits arising from its democratization and constitutionalization.

utive discretion and the idea of limited government, but those tensions do not represent an irreconcilable conflict. The development of liberal democratic theory is characterized by a growing recognition of a need for discretionary executive authority and of the executive's need for sensitivity to popular will in a limited government based on consent.

To recover a more balanced conception of liberal political theory, it is first necessary to identify the source of our contemporary confusion. By looking closely at the political theories of Machiavelli, Hobbes, Locke, and Montesquieu, we find the origin of the arguments defending broad extralegal discretion on the part of the executive, as well as of arguments that identify modern liberal government with the rule of law and the doctrine of legislative supremacy. But we shall also see that early modern political theory is not constituted by a simple progressive evolution from the preoccupation with political power and executive authority of Machiavelli and Hobbes to the recognition of the virtues of political liberty, legislative supremacy, and checks and balances in the writings of Locke and Montesquieu. The defenders of executive discretion, and the defenders of legislative supremacy, do not form two opposing camps. They are joined together in a common cause.

ON FIRST READING

Origins of the Strong Executive

Machiavelli and Hobbes are the most prominent defenders of executive power in modern political thought. In Machiavelli's *Prince* we find a guide for the exercise of power by a prince, and in Hobbes's *Leviathan* we find a justification for the acceptance by the people of an authoritative absolute sovereign.[3]

3. My first reading obviously represents an incomplete account or interpretation of the texts involved. Furthermore, I do not mean to ascribe this interpretation to any particular author. I am not, however, merely fabricating a weak argument, which I can then easily refute. I am attempting to create a view of early modern political philosophy from the perspective of a whig view of government. It is necessary to do this because most contemporary commentators on the separation of powers do not present a comprehensive analysis of the early modern political thinkers who provide the foundations for the modern doctrine of executive power. For example, even such classic works on the separation of powers as M. J. C. Vile's *Constitutionalism and the Separation of Powers* (New York: Oxford University Press, 1967) provide no analysis of the relationship between Machiavelli's prince or Hobbes's sovereign and the modern executive.

Following this initial reading, I look at these early modern political theorists from two

The Prince is written from the perspective of the self-interest of the ruler. It explains the most effective means of maintaining power. Although recent scholars have attempted to emphasize republican elements in Machiavelli's writings, the meaning of Machiavellianism in the minds of most people remains quite clear.[4] A Machiavellian is manipulative, self-serving, and if not immoral at least amoral.

There is good reason for this belief. Machiavelli explicitly states that he is interested not in goodness but in the necessities of rule:

> A man who wants to make a profession of good in all regards must come to ruin among so many who are not good. Hence it is necessary to a prince, if he wants to maintain himself, to learn to be able not to be good, and to use this and not use it according to necessity.[5]

Success, not goodness, is the standard that guides Machiavelli's prince. In what is perhaps the most famous passage in *The Prince*, Machiavelli counsels the ruler to seek success by imitating the lion and the fox:

> Since a prince is compelled of necessity to know well how to use the beast, he should pick the fox and the lion, because the lion does not defend itself from snares and the fox does not defend itself

---

additional perspectives. My three readings of these thinkers is somewhat analogous to the approach of Graham Allison in *Essence of Decision* (Boston: Little, Brown & Co., 1971). Allison created three different explanations of the Cuban missile crisis based on three different assumptions about the character of decision-making. He knew that each of these three approaches was incomplete, but he believed that by isolating and developing these different approaches we would be better able to see how our different assumptions would lead to different understandings of the event. I hope that my three readings of the early modern theorists will make the assumptions underlying the different contemporary theories of the separation of powers clearer.

    4. The obvious exception to this argument is found in the civic republican school led by J. G. A. Pocock. Pocock sees Machiavelli's writings as a revitalization of the classical republican tradition of Aristotle. See J. G. A. Pocock, *The Machiavellian Moment* (Princeton: Princeton University Press, 1975). In making his case, however, he ignores the harsher side of Machiavelli's teaching and in many cases simply ignores Machiavelli's arguments in favor of an examination of Machiavelli's historical context. The text of Machiavelli's works is overwhelmed by the context. For an explanation of this problem in Pocock, see Vickie B. Sullivan, "Machiavelli's Momentary 'Machiavellian Moment': A Reconsideration of Pocock's Treatment of the Discourses," in *Political Theory* 20 (May 1992), 309–18. Although Pocock's view enjoys a current popularity, it has not been able to change the generally accepted meaning of the term "Machiavellian."

    5. Niccolò Machiavelli, *The Prince*, trans. Harvey C. Mansfield Jr. (Chicago: University of Chicago Press, 1985), 61.

from wolves. So one needs to be a fox to recognize snares and a lion to frighten wolves.[6]

The role of the lion is immediately obvious to the reader of *The Prince*. Machiavelli points out the harsh realities a successful ruler must face. He is often shocking in his open advocacy of the use of force and even cruelty. In chapter 17 of *The Prince* he contends that a ruler should not be concerned with a reputation for cruelty. In fact, "it is much safer to be feared than loved." Men are "ungrateful, fickle pretenders and dissemblers, evaders of danger, eager for gain." Love is based on a sense of obligation, a sense that disappears after a good deed has been performed. Fear, however, is based on the dread of punishment, a dread that the prince can always call forth.[7]

This is the reasoning that leads Machiavelli to remind his readers that a few well-timed executions can do much to maintain the peace and stability of the community.[8] He even claims it is better to kill a subject's father than to take away the subject's property. The former appears to be more cruel, but it will be more quickly forgotten. A man will adjust more easily to life without his father than he will to life without his property.[9] These are the harsh truths of the rule of the lion.

The rule of the fox appears to be an alternative to the rule of force. Machiavelli explains that it is good to have the reputation for virtue.[10] The people will be more willing to accept the rule of a prince they perceive to be "good." As long as the prince remains clear on the necessity for cruelty, it is acceptable, even desirable, for him to present an image of virtue. He goes on to explain that rulers should willingly make promises to their subjects that they have no intention of keeping.[11] That is perhaps why Machiavelli has earlier claimed that the wise prince will even accept the rule of law in certain circumstances.[12] The laws constitute a promise, a promise that can be kept as long as it is in the interest of the prince to do so. The laws help the prince to govern by making his actions more acceptable to the people, but he must be willing to ignore the laws when his interest requires him to do so.

Machiavelli provides a similar justification for the creation of such institutions as the French parliament. He says that the ruler who created the

6. Ibid., 69.
7. Ibid., 66–67.
8. Ibid., 65–66.
9. Ibid., 67.
10. Ibid., 70.
11. Ibid., 69–70.
12. Ibid., 20.

French parliament recognized that rich and powerful men would be ambitious, and that the poor would resent and fear the rich and powerful. If the king tried to restrain the ambition of the rich or to mediate between the rich and the poor, he would incur the hatred of the rich when he favored the poor, and the hatred of the poor when he favored the rich. The parliament was established to create a new force that would "beat down the great and favor the lesser side without blame for the king."[13] The king benefits by enlisting the aid of the poor to check the ambition of the rich, who would be the greatest threat to his power. But he benefits in another sense as well. The king does not have to directly control the rich. The parliament does the job for him, and thereby deflects any resentment he might incur if he sought more direct control. The fox allows others to perform the undesirable tasks of government.

The fox rules by indirection, but we should not be deceived into believing that his rule is less bestial. Machiavelli provides a most revealing example of what he considers to be the proper relationship between the rule of the lion and the rule of the fox. He relates the story of Severus, who had moved his troops into Rome, killed the Emperor Julianus, and was elected emperor by the Senate. Severus wanted to consolidate his power, but there were two men who posed a threat—Pescennius Niger, head of the Asian armies, and Albinius, head of the western armies. He decided to deal with Niger using the methods of the lion, and with Albinius using the methods of the fox. He told Albinius that he wanted to share power with him, and at the same time he attacked Niger. After defeating Niger and putting him to death, he returned to Rome, where he accused Albinius of plotting to kill him. Under this pretext he "took from him his state and his life."[14]

Machiavelli has led us to believe that this story illustrates the need for both the fox and the lion, and in one sense it does. Severus could not have immediately acted as a lion in regard to both Niger and Albinius. He needed to use the methods of the fox in at least one case. But those methods were used primarily to buy time. Albinius meets the same bloody end as Niger. The real teaching of the story is that it may sometimes be necessary for the lion to hide behind the fox. In the end, however, the law of the jungle prevails. The lion and the fox are both beasts, and the rule they live by is to kill or be killed. The prince must learn to face the harsh

---

13. Ibid., 75. Although the French parliament of which Machiavelli spoke was more of a judicial than a legislative body, the argument would apply with equal weight to an essentially legislative body.

14. Ibid., 78–79. Another example of the successful prince using the arms of others is Cesare Borgia's use of Messer Remirro to subdue Romagna in chapter 7, pp. 29–30.

realities of rule, even if it is often useful to disguise those realities when dealing with his subjects.

Machiavelli concludes *The Prince* with a call to action. He admits that men may not always be able to conquer fortune, but if they are bold he holds out the hope for some success. In a passage that can easily be read as a praise of rape, Machiavelli claims:

> It is better to be impetuous than cautious, because fortune is a woman; and it is necessary, if one wants to hold her down, to beat her and strike her down. And one sees that she lets herself be won by the impetuous [rather] than by those who proceed coldly. And so always, like a woman, she is the friend of the young, because they are less cautious, more ferocious, and command her with more audacity.

To rule successfully, one must be ferocious and command with audacity.

Machiavelli's *Prince* provides clear advice to the ruler on the maintenance of power, but it says little about the reasons the people would accept such a cynical and ruthless form of rule. The most apparent answer in *The Prince* is fear of the ruler. Hobbes's *Leviathan* accepts that reason, but it provides an additional one: fear of the alternative to the arbitrary rule of a prince. Hobbes argues that the people are better off under the rule of an absolute sovereign than they would be in the absence of such a ruler.

Hobbes claims that the alternative to an absolute sovereign is the state of nature, where life is "solitary, poor, nasty, brutish and short."[15] In the state of nature, "every man has a right to every thing; even to one another's body." As long as man stays in this natural state, "there can be no security to any man, how strong or wise soever he be."[16]

According to Hobbes, the only way to escape the insecurity of the state of nature is to enter into a social contract, whereby each man "lay[s] down his right to all things; and be contented with so much liberty against other men, as he would allow other men against himself."[17] But one cannot rely on the goodwill of other people to enforce such a contract. The social contract must create a sovereign capable of enforcing the contract.

The power of the sovereign must be beyond question. There is no contract between the sovereign and the people that establishes the limits of rule, because there could be no power superior to the sovereign capable

---

15. Thomas Hobbes, *Leviathan* (New York: Macmillan Co., 1962), 100.
16. Ibid., 103.
17. Ibid., 104.

of enforcing such a contract.[18] The contract is really an expansion of the role of law in *The Prince*. In *The Prince* the laws legitimate or make more acceptable the particular actions of the prince. In the *Leviathan* the social contract legitimizes the general rule of the sovereign. The contract gives legitimacy to the sovereign's actions, but it does not appear to protect the subjects from the sovereign. Hobbes makes it clear that the sovereign can do whatever he deems necessary to maintain the peace and security of the commonwealth.

Hobbes provides a detailed list of the necessary rights of the sovereign. First, the subjects cannot rid themselves of the sovereign without his permission. To do so would break the covenant they made with one another and return them to a state of nature. If the sovereign is not absolutely secure in his authority, there would be no power capable of settling all disputes that may arise within the commonwealth.[19] Furthermore, the subjects may not accuse the sovereign of injustice. The sovereign is created by the people, and every action he performs is therefore the will of the people. Thus Hobbes concludes that it is impossible for the sovereign to act unjustly.[20] The sovereign must be the final judge in all matters of conduct; he may even determine "what doctrines are fit to be taught."[21]

Hobbes's chapter on the liberty of subjects paradoxically provides a strong case for the authority of the sovereign. For example, early in the chapter Hobbes argues that fear and liberty are consistent. Although subjects obey the sovereign out of fear they do so freely:

> When a man throweth his goods into the sea for fear the ship should sink, he doth it nevertheless very willingly, and may refuse to do it if he will: it is therefore the action of one that was free.[22]

Hobbes even contends that being put to death by the sovereign is consistent with liberty. The reason for this is that "every subject is author of every act of the sovereign."[23] The absolute authority of the sovereign is not only consistent with liberty, according to Hobbes, it is absolutely necessary for liberty to exist. Without such authority man is returned to the state of nature, where he can never be secure in his rights.

There can be no doubt that Machiavelli and Hobbes stress the need for a powerful ruler to maintain a stable political system. Political order is clearly at the forefront of their political teachings.

18. Ibid., 135.
19. Ibid., 134.
20. Ibid., 136.
21. Ibid., 137.
22. Ibid., 159–60.
23. Ibid., 161.

The Origins of Legislative Supremacy and the Separation of Powers

It is precisely this preoccupation with political order that is rejected in the name of democracy and freedom by later modern thinkers such as Locke and Montesquieu. It is therefore Locke and Montesquieu, and not Machiavelli and Hobbes, who are usually cited in association with the founding of the American political system.[24]

Locke explicitly rejects the idea of an absolute sovereign and calls instead for a government based on consent and structured according to the idea of legislative supremacy. Locke contends that individual freedom and consent are inconsistent with the rule of an absolute sovereign. There are limits to the powers of government:

> For no body can transfer to another more power than he has himself; and no body has an absolute power over himself, or over any other, to destroy his own life, or take away the life or property of another. A man, as has been proved, cannot subject himself to the arbitrary will of another.[25]

Men enter into society in order to receive the benefits of liberty. If society required the acquiescence in the rule of an absolute sovereign, then the means would conflict with the end of government.

According to Locke, the supreme power in every commonwealth is the legislature. The legislature represents the will of the people, which is the only legitimate sovereign authority. Through the legislature, consent is

---

24. Scholars see the theories of Locke and Montesquieu as closer to the American political tradition than those of Machiavelli or Hobbes, and they also tend to depreciate any influence of Machiavelli and Hobbes on the works of these later thinkers. For example, Peter Laslett identifies Locke as a whig theorist who believes in legislative supremacy, and he devotes an entire section of his introduction to an argument that Locke was responding to Filmer rather than Hobbes. See John Locke, *Two Treatises of Government,* introduction and notes by Peter Laslett (New York: New American Library, 1965), 80–92. By denying Hobbes the role of Locke's major opponent, Laslett seeks to minimize any theoretical link between the writings of Hobbes and Locke.

As Harvey Mansfield has pointed out, commentators such as M. J. C. Vile and W. B. Gwyn find the antecedents of Locke's separation of the legislative and executive powers in the English civil war. See Vile, *Constitutionalism and the Separation of Powers,* 58; W. B. Gwyn, *The Meaning of the Separation of Powers* (New Orleans, La.: Tulane Studies in Political Science, 1965), chaps. 3, 4; Harvey Mansfield Jr., "The Modern Doctrine of Executive Power," *Presidential Studies Quarterly* 17 (Spring 1987), 295. Thus they trace the origins of a distinct executive power to a desire to limit such power.

25. Locke, *Two Treatises,* 402.

exercised continuously in the operation of government, not just in its establishment. Moreover, the legislature does not govern arbitrarily, but governs through law. Through laws "the people may know their duty, and be safe and secure within the limits of the law, and the rulers too kept within their due bounds, and not be tempted by the power they have in their hands."[26] The laws are the expression of the will of the people made through the legislature. For Locke, legislative supremacy and the rule of law are the means to self-government.

Under such a system the executive is not an absolute sovereign; he is a necessary tool for carrying out the will of the people as expressed by the legislature. He rules not according to a general mandate to maintain the peace and security of the community, but in pursuance of specific laws passed by the legislature in the name of the people:

> [No] edict of anybody else, in what form soever conceived, or by what power soever backed, [has] the force and obligation of a law, which has not its sanction from the [legislature] which the public has chosen and appointed.[27]

The executive exists as a matter of convenience. "The laws that are at once, and in a short time made, have a constant and lasting force, and need a perpetual execution."[28] The work of the legislature requires only a limited time, but there must be some force constantly capable of executing the legislature's will once it has been established. Such an executive has little claim to independent discretionary authority. He is obviously intended to be a servant of the legislature.

Montesquieu accepts Locke's contention that liberty is the end of government. He defines liberty as "a tranquility of mind arising from the opinion each person has of his safety."[29] Government should make citizens feel secure in the exercise of their rights. But Montesquieu takes Locke's argument a step further. Although Locke separates the legislative and executive powers, it is Montesquieu who makes the separation of powers a cornerstone of his political theory. He criticizes the concentration of the powers of government even if it is in a legislative assembly. Montesquieu contends: "When the legislative and executive powers are united in the same person, or in the same body of magistrates, there can be no liberty."[30]

26. Ibid., 406.

27. Ibid., 400.

28. Ibid., 410.

29. Montesquieu, *The Spirit of the Laws,* trans. Thomas Nugent (New York: Hafner Press, 1949), 151.

30. Ibid. Madison quotes this statement in *Federalist* No. 47. See Alexander Hamilton et al., *The Federalist,* ed. Jacob E. Cooke (Cleveland: Meridian Books, 1961), 324.

Liberty is the end of government, and unchecked political power is the greatest threat to liberty. Montesquieu therefore calls for a separation of powers to protect against the arbitrary exercise of power. Montesquieu is not hostile to the legislature, nor in this view does he have any particular regard for the executive; he simply doesn't trust any concentration of power. The executive exists because it serves as a check on the legislature, and he in turn will be checked by the legislature. Montesquieu reacts even more strongly than Locke to the fear of absolute sovereignty.

Montesquieu also claims that "there is no liberty if the judiciary power be not separated from the legislature and the executive."[31] The judicial power is the power most to be feared by the citizens, for it is the power that punishes individuals. An independent judiciary protects the rights of the citizens from the arbitrary exercise of power.

> Were [the judicial power] joined with the legislature, the life and liberty of the subject would be exposed to arbitrary control; for the judge would be the legislator. Were it joined to the executive power, the judge might behave with violence and oppression.[32]

In Montesquieu's scheme the citizens will not be subject to the whims of legislatures, which make the general rules, or to the executive who arrests them. They will be tried by an independent judiciary, which will include a jury of their peers. Thus Montesquieu's executive is restrained by a legislature that passes the laws and by a judiciary that will apply the laws in individual cases.

Not only does Montesquieu protect individual rights through the independent judiciary, he also provides the most explicit argument for the concept of a bill of rights. He discusses a number of restrictions that should be placed on the power of government to punish individual citizens. For example, a person should not be condemned to death unless two witnesses testify against him.[33] A person should not be punished for his religious beliefs, unless his actions in some way directly threaten the tranquility of the state.[34] And freedom of speech is defended on the grounds that "Words do not constitute an overt act; they remain only an idea."[35] According to Montesquieu, these limitations must be accepted if the liberty of the subject is to be secure. Liberty requires a separation of powers, an

31. Montesquieu, *Spirit of the Laws*, 152.
32. Ibid.
33. Ibid., 184.
34. Ibid., 185–87.
35. Ibid., 193.

independent judiciary, and the explicit statement of certain individual rights.

It is this view of Locke and Montesquieu which informs much of the contemporary discussion of the theory of executive power and of liberal government. The separation of powers is seen only as a check on the abuse of power. Popular government rests on the principle of legislative supremacy. A powerful and independent executive is considered the product of an excessive concern with stability and power and is an idea more closely related to monarchy than to popular government.

ON SECOND READING

The Liberal Assumptions of Hobbes and Machiavelli

Our initial reading stands, however, only if we ignore a substantial amount of evidence for an alternative interpretation. No matter how powerful the rulers proposed by Machiavelli and Hobbes, it is nonetheless clear that those rulers are to operate within the context of a modern liberal state. The selfishness of Machiavelli's prince is not the selfishness of an ancient tyrant. The maintenance of power, not the plunder or utter subjugation of the citizens, is the goal of the prince.

Machiavelli teaches that while princes should be feared they should not be hated. He even says that it is helpful for the prince to be loved. To avoid hatred, Machiavelli warns, princes must respect certain rights of their citizens. The prince must abstain "from the property of his citizens and his subjects, and from their women; and if he . . . needs to proceed against someone's life, he must do it when there is suitable justification."[36] It is strange indeed to hear Machiavelli suggest a basis for the recognition of individual rights. To be sure, Machiavelli is making the argument in the name of what is expedient for the ruler, and not in terms of the inalienable rights of the people. Nonetheless, the effect is the same. The people will enjoy a certain security under the rule of Machiavelli's prince. The prince will be careful "not to make the great desperate and . . . to satisfy the people and keep them content, because this is one of the most important matters that concern a prince."[37] If the people like the prince, it will be easier for him to maintain his rule. The interests of the people and the prince may not be quite so much at odds with each other as one would

36. *The Prince*, 67.
37. Ibid., 74.

think on first reading. A stable and peaceful state is good for the prince, but it is also good for the people. Peace and stability are prerequisites for individual happiness.

It also should be remembered that if the people disagree with the prince about the best interests of the state, the people have a great deal of power to check the prince; they outnumber him and can destroy him. Machiavelli constantly reminds the prince that the greatest danger to his rule comes from the hatred of the people. He even concludes his discussion of the importance of fortresses with the claim that he "shall blame anyone who, trusting in fortresses, thinks little of being hated by the people."[38] The prince will survive only to the extent that he convinces the citizens that he has protected the state from external dangers and that he has provided a safe and secure domestic life. His claim to rule rests not on divine right or traditional natural law, but on the effective exercise of political power. He is a true modern liberal ruler.

The liberal basis of Hobbes's political teaching is even more readily apparent. Although there can be no enforceable contract between the sovereign and the people, the existence of the social contract in Hobbes's commonwealth is a constant reminder both to the sovereign and to the people that the foundation of the sovereign's power is the doctrine of individual rights. It is surprising to note that Hobbes is the first liberal political thinker to present a doctrine of inalienable rights. He claims:

> Not all rights are alienable. Whensoever a man transferreth his right, or renounceth it; it is either in consideration of some right reciprocally transferred to himself; or for some other good he hopeth for thereby. For it is a voluntary act: and of the voluntary acts of every man, the object is some good to himself.[39]

The creation of the sovereign is a voluntary act aimed at the good of those who joined in inaugurating the social contract. The social contract makes explicit what was implicit in *The Prince:* the dependence of the sovereign on the people.

Although it is Locke and not Hobbes who is usually credited with originating the idea of a right to revolution, Hobbes explicitly states that the individual is the one who must judge when he is secure in his rights. The sovereign, for example, has the right to punish or kill a subject whose view of his own rights comes into conflict with the sovereign's view of the good of the state. However, the individual whose life is threatened is no

38. Ibid., 87.
39. *Leviathan,* 105.

longer subject to the social contract, and he is free to resist the sovereign. Hobbes even extends this concept to a right against self-incrimination. Just as the subject has the right to resist a death sentence from the sovereign, the sovereign has no right to force someone to condemn himself from his own lips.[40] Finally Hobbes argues that individuals who fear that their lives are in danger from the sovereign have a right to join together to resist the sovereign.[41] It would be difficult indeed for the sovereign to distinguish such a group from a revolutionary movement.

The greatest liberty is not, however, to be found in the right to resist the sovereign. According to Hobbes, "the greatest liberty of subjects, dependeth on the silence of the law."[42] Hobbes explains: "In cases where the sovereign has prescribed no rule, there the subject hath the liberty to do, or forbear, according to his own discretion."[43] Hobbes admits that in some cases and in some times this area of freedom will be greater than in others. But the assumption behind this view of liberty is that much of life will remain outside the power of the sovereign. The sovereign cannot prescribe rules for every aspect of life. Moreover, he has no reason to try to do so. He need only regulate private life to the extent that is necessary to maintain the peace and security of the commonwealth. In a commonwealth where the law permits whatever is not expressly forbidden, there is inevitably much room for freedom.

The liberal foundations of the writings of Machiavelli and Hobbes cannot be ignored or denied. The remainder of their political teaching must be seen in terms of this foundation.

Political Power in Locke and Montesquieu

Regardless of Locke's and Montesquieu's explicit emphasis on popular control, legislative supremacy, and checks and balances, much in their writing suggests support for a strong and independent executive.

For example, Locke explicitly calls for legislative supremacy, but a close examination of Locke's teaching on the executive reveals some rather surprising qualifications on legislative supremacy. The federative power, the power to conduct foreign policy, is given to the executive. This is not a limited power to deal with emergencies but the power to act in the name of the nation in dealing with other nations. It is not a power to be directed by the legislature or the laws because "what is to be done in reference to

40. Ibid., 164.
41. Ibid., 165.
42. Ibid.
43. Ibid., 166.

Foreigners, depending much upon their actions, and the variation of designs and interests, must be left in great part to the Prudence of those who have this power committed to them, to be managed by the best of their Skill, for the advantage of the Commonwealth."[44] The executive, not the legislature, is the branch of government most able to direct the force of the commonwealth in the varied and constantly changing circumstances of foreign affairs.

The doctrine of prerogative is related to domestic policy. Although it is frequently seen as an exceptional power to deal with emergencies, its limitations are not so clear. Locke begins his discussion of the doctrine of prerogative with this claim:

> The Legislators not being able to foresee, and provide, by Laws, for all that may be useful to the Community, the Executor of the Laws, having the power in his hands, has by the common Law of Nature, a right to make use of it, for the good of Society, in many cases, where the municipal Law has given no direction, till the legislature can be conveniently assembled to provide for it.[45]

This would appear to be a relatively modest power based on the fact that the legislature is not always in session. The executive can act on his own, until such time as the legislature can make its will known on a given issue. But Locke continues his discussion with this claim:

> Many things there are, which the Law can by no means provide for, and those must be left to the discretion of him that has the Executive Power in his hands, to be ordered by him as the public good and advantage may require.[46]

There are certain acts of governing that the legislature can never direct or control. Finally Locke argues: " 'Tis fit that the Laws themselves should in some cases give way to the executive power."[47] Thus the doctrine of prerogative supports the executive claim to supersede the laws of the legislature.

It is certainly difficult to understand the meaning of legislative supremacy in this context. The executive may act in the absence of legislative authority. He may act contrary to legislative authority. The only qualifi-

44. *Two Treatises*, 412.
45. Ibid., 420.
46. Ibid.
47. Ibid., 421.

cation is that the executive must decide that such action is in the public interest. This does not seem very different from Hobbes's sovereign.

The executive can also place some important restrictions on the legislature. He can convene and adjourn the legislature at will.[48] He can reapportion the legislature according to what he deems to be a more just apportionment.[49] Moreover, the executive cannot be removed by the legislature. In fact, he can be removed only by an appeal to heaven.[50]

A reexamination of Montesquieu's writings also reveals important qualifications on the principles of legislative supremacy, checks and balances, and popular control. Montesquieu distinguishes between modern liberal government and ancient participatory democracies. In fact, Montesquieu rejects ancient democracy as a model. He declares that virtue is the spring of ancient democracy, but he goes on to point out the unreliability of virtue as a basis for sound government.[51]

When Montesquieu begins his discussion of modern liberal government, he immediately rejects democracy as a standard: "It is true that in democracies the people seem to act as they please; but political liberty does not consist in an unlimited freedom."[52] The rule of law, not participatory democracy, is the standard of liberty held up by Montesquieu.[53] A man cannot be free without law. Montesquieu explains: "Liberty is the right of doing whatever the laws permit, and if a citizen could do what they forbid he would no longer be possessed of liberty, because all of his fellow-citizens would have the same power."[54] Only under the rule of law are citizens genuinely free, because only under the rule of law are they secure in their rights.

It should be noted that the primary importance of the rule of law is not its expression of popular will. Montesquieu defends the rule of law because it is a means to ordered liberty. The legislators are not to be mere spokespersons for popular opinion. According to Montesquieu, the legislators are superior to the body of the people in determining policy. It would be undesirable, even if possible, for legislators to seek the advice of the people on each particular issue.[55] This is why Montesquieu concludes

48. Ibid., 417.
49. Ibid., 419.
50. Ibid., 476.
51. *Spirit of the Laws*, 20.
52. Ibid., 150.
53. The distinction between liberal republicanism and participatory democracy in *Spirit of the Laws* is explained most fully in Thomas Pangle, *Montesquieu's Philosophy of Liberalism: A Commentary on "The Spirit of the Laws"* (Chicago: University of Chicago Press, 1973), esp. chaps. 4, 5.
54. *Spirit of the Laws*, 150.
55. Ibid., 154.

that one of the great faults of ancient democracies was the right of the people directly to pass laws.[56] Montesquieu takes great pains to distinguish between democracy and liberal government.

Although Montesquieu is surprisingly critical of ancient democracy, he finds much to praise in monarchy: "In monarchies policy effects great things with as little virtue as possible. Thus in the nicest machines art has reduced the number of movements, springs and wheels."[57] Monarchy avoids the major defect of democracy; it does not rely on virtue for its success. The spring of monarchy is honor: "Honor sets all parts of the body politic in motion, and by its very action connects them; thus each individual advances the public good, while he only thinks of his own interest."[58] Thus monarchy encourages people "to perform the most difficult actions" by promising them only "glory and applause."[59] It is monarchy that gives birth to the liberal conception of the invisible hand, in which persons pursuing their own interests will ultimately serve the public good.

Montesquieu recognized that there will be a tendency in modern liberal governments for power to become concentrated in the legislature. That is why he is so concerned with providing a firm foundation for executive power. Montesquieu calls for an executive power to be placed in the hands of a monarch, because "this branch of government having need of dispatch is better administered by one than by many."[60]

The executive must have a veto power over legislation, because without such a veto "the legislative body would become despotic." Montesquieu accepts many of Locke's other proposals for controlling the legislature. Montesquieu says the legislature should meet only when and for as long as the executive deems appropriate. He also argues that whereas the executive should be able to restrain the legislature, "the legislature should not have the right to stay the executive." Montesquieu goes on to say that there are natural limits to the executive power, but it is clear that the legislature has no right to determine the precise character of those limits or to enforce them. The person of the executive is to be "sacred." "The moment he is accused or tried there is an end to liberty."[61] Montesquieu sees no conflict between an inviolable executive and his conception of liberty.

What is perhaps most surprising, however, is that Montesquieu recognizes a place for despotic elements in his liberal government. The arbitrary

56. Ibid., 155.
57. Ibid., 23.
58. Ibid., 25. One cannot help being reminded of *Federalist* No. 51, where Madison argues that we should use ambition as a substitute for virtue (*The Federalist*, 349).
59. *Spirit of the Laws*, 25.
60. Ibid., 156.
61. Ibid., 158.

despot is the very antithesis of the liberal principle of the rule of law. The despot rules not by means of law but by means of fear.[62] But Montesquieu finds room even for fear in his liberal constitution.

Montesquieu recognizes that the element of fear must be present in all governments. Otherwise, the laws would not be observed. The danger is that fear of government will lead the citizens to distrust the government. The creation of an independent judicial power represents Montesquieu's attempt to find an acceptable place for fear within the context of a liberal polity. Montesquieu says that the judicial power "should be exercised by persons taken from the body of the people at certain times of the year . . . in order to erect a tribunal that should last only so long as necessity requires." A system of trial by jury will diminish the fear of the people. The virtue of such a system is that the "people have not the judges continually present in their view; they fear the office but not the magistrate." "The judicial power, so terrible to mankind, . . . becomes, as it were, invisible."[63] The people do not fear and distrust what they do not see.

This system is particularly beneficial to the executive. In Locke's commonwealth there is no distinction between executive and judicial power. The power "so terrible to mankind" is wielded by the executive. But in wielding such a power the executive himself must become terrible to the people. By removing this terrible power from the executive branch, Montesquieu indirectly enhances the executive's power. The laws will continue to be enforced and the people punished. As in the teachings of Machiavelli and Hobbes, sovereign authority will be maintained by fear, but the fear will not be directly attributable to the executive.[64] The wise executive will rule indirectly, like the fox, by using the laws and the judiciary to perform the unpleasant tasks of government. As Montesquieu explains in a passage that might well have come from the pen of Machiavelli: "the prince ought only to encourage, and let the laws menace."[65]

A MORE COMPLETE VIEW

How does one reconcile these two readings of Machiavelli, Hobbes, Locke, and Montesquieu? Perhaps they appear more at odds than they

---

62. Ibid., 26.
63. Ibid., 153.
64. Mansfield makes a similar point (*Taming the Prince*, 234–35).
65. *Spirit of the Laws*, 203.

are, precisely because we have come to accept the assumption that a strong executive or any form of discretionary political authority is inconsistent with the principles of liberal government. We need to begin with an alternative assumption and see whether it can explain more. The assumption we should now explore is that liberal government and a strong executive are dependent on each other and may even be constructed so that they enhance rather than threaten each other.

The mutual dependence of liberty and executive power can be seen in the writings of Machiavelli and Hobbes. Much of the inconsistency between our first two readings disappears if we recognize the context in which these authors were writing. We are not talking just about the particular political context of the divided Italy of Machiavelli or the religious civil wars of Hobbes's England. The broader context was the breakdown of traditional sources of political authority, such as divine right and traditional notions of aristocracy and natural law. Machiavelli and Hobbes were concerned that any political system would be unstable without such supports, that domestic anarchy or civil war would threaten from within, and that a stronger more unified power would threaten from without.

Neither Machiavelli nor Hobbes sought a return to the past. They did not try to resurrect divine right or traditional aristocratic ideas. Instead they accepted and elaborated the idea of individual liberty as a basis for a political system. They realized that it would not be difficult to have the people accept this principle, but it would be difficult to get the people to see that once this principle was accepted political authority would still be necessary—in fact, more necessary.

Liberal government can survive and prosper only if the people are willing to accept effective political authority. This is the case that must be made most forcefully. However, this teaching should in no way diminish the importance of their quieter teaching to rulers, that in the future political power will rest on the ability of the ruler to make the people feel secure in the exercise of their rights. Political authority and executive power are not the enemies of liberal government; they are its necessary allies. If Machiavelli and Hobbes sought to show the mutual dependence of executive power and liberal government, Locke and Montesquieu tried to establish their mutual compatibility. There was no disagreement between Locke and Montesquieu, on the one hand, and Machiavelli and Hobbes, on the other hand, about the interdependence of executive power and liberal government. Locke and Montesquieu saw clearly and accepted the proposition that the modern liberal state would require a strong executive, who would exercise discretionary authority, and the proposition that modern rulers must found their claim to rule on some form of popular support.

The problem with Hobbes's commonwealth was that although the mutual dependence of these principles was demonstrated, the potential for conflict was demonstrated too. The people would fear an all-powerful sovereign, who would be perceived as a more immediate threat to their rights than the state of nature. Indeed, he might be such a threat if the key to political stability was his maintenance of his unquestioned political authority. The people would be jealous of their rights, and in a system where their only choices were the acceptance of the absolute authority of the sovereign or a return to the state of nature, the legitimacy of the sovereign's rule would continually be in question.

Locke and Montesquieu understood that the reduction of this conflict would enhance both individual liberty and effective government. Thus they sought to create institutional structures that would bridge the gap between the people and government. Locke's legislature clearly serves that purpose. It expands the idea of consent and allows it to function not just in the establishment of government but also in its ongoing operation. The legislature represents the opinion of the individual citizens who finally hold the sovereign power. This is what Locke means by legislative supremacy.

But executive power may also be enhanced by this development. The existence of the legislature provides additional legitimacy to actions of the executive. While the laws may limit government action, they may also provide tools for governing. Furthermore, the legislature provides the executive with information about the opinions of the people, and also provides an outlet for their dissatisfactions, short of the right of revolution. Finally, the executive is given the power to do what is necessary to maintain the peace and security of the community, and it is still the executive who will perform the actual tasks of governing. The legislature can pass laws that restrict action, but it cannot act.

Montesquieu's judiciary performs a similar function. Just as the legislature provides a bridge between the people and the government through the creation of laws, the judiciary, particularly the system of trial by jury, provides a link between the people and the government in the application of the law to individuals. Individual rights are given additional protection by the creation of an independent judiciary. At the same time, the executive can safely be given sufficient power to execute the laws, because his actions will be circumscribed by the existence of an independent judiciary.

In the system designed by Locke and Montesquieu, the contest between liberty and authority is not a zero-sum game. One does not gain only at the expense of the other. To the contrary, it would appear that the gains of each must come together.

THE PROBLEM OF LIBERAL GOVERNMENT

The problem of the liberal executive is really synonymous with the problem of liberal government: How are individual rights and the need for political authority to be reconciled? The founders of modern liberal government, however, saw not just a problem but also an opportunity. They did not deny that tension exists. There is a mutual threat. But if there is a conflict there is also a mutual dependence. No one would be secure in the exercise of his rights without a political authority capable of enforcing those rights. No political authority would survive if it ignored the opinions and interests of its citizens. The problem began to emerge as an opportunity when liberal thinkers saw that the potential for mutual enhancement was perhaps greater than the potential for conflict. Would not the difficulty of ruling be reduced if the ends of rule were limited? If less was expected of politics, would more be accomplished? The prince and the sovereign are told to maximize their political power, but they are constantly reminded by Machiavelli and Hobbes not to make their job any more difficult than necessary. If the actions of the citizens are no threat to the state, then they need be of no interest to the government. If the citizens feel secure in their rights, then they will have no reason to pose a threat to the sovereign or the prince. Also, would not the people be more secure in their rights in a stable and effectively governed political order? Would they not be more free to exercise their rights if the political system provided an environment in which they were protected from internal and external conflict? Is not political stability as much a boon to the people as to the ruler? As in a good marriage, conflict is not eliminated, but it is submerged under the benefits that flow from the union.

This union would not have been possible, or at least it would not have been so harmonious without the development of independent executive, legislative, and judicial powers. As has been argued, the development of these separate branches has helped to lessen the conflict between government and citizens. The legislature has institutionalized the role of consent in government. The judiciary has served to insulate the individual from the arbitrary enforcement of executive power and the arbitrary will of the legislature. The executive has demonstrated the possibility of providing adequate government power within a context that is conducive to liberty.

But it is also important to return to the origins of liberal government to understand the different origins of the different branches. The legislature does not grow out of Machiavelli's prince or Hobbes's sovereign, it grows out of the principle of consent. This fact has important implications for the way in which we understand legislative power and its role in liberal government. Because consent provides the foundation for liberal government, it is easy to see why Locke speaks of legislative supremacy. But we must also remember that there is a difference between consent and rule. Consent is the permission to act; rule is action. The legislature does not just give consent, it also passes laws, but it is impossible for laws to rule either. Laws provide the limits and the tools of ruling, but they can neither interpret nor enforce themselves. Nor can they cover all possible circumstances. Laws inevitably leave room for the exercise of discretion.

To recognize these facts is not to diminish the importance of the legislature, but it is to recognize something important about the character of legislative power. It is a power that can only be exercised indirectly. The legislature helps to lessen the gap between consent and rule, but it does not eliminate that gap.

The judiciary's origins are more ambiguous. In Locke the judiciary was a part of the executive, and the development of an independent judiciary could be seen as mere subdivision of the executive power. From this perspective the judge might find a solid basis on which to claim broad discretionary authority, for the origins of the judiciary could be traced to the inadequacies of the rule of law. The judge, like the executive, could be seen as a necessary supplement to the rule of law. He would use his discretionary authority to protect the individual and to ensure that justice is done in particular cases.

But the judges' claim to authority rests in part on the doctrine of the rule of law. The judge personifies the law. He embodies the neutral principles of justice inherent in the concept of the rule of law. The legitimacy of the judge rests at least partially on the belief that he acts not to impose his own will but as a spokesperson for the law. He gives life to the law, but he does not use the law as a mere tool to give legal weight to his own personal opinions.

It is obvious that these two views of the judiciary are in conflict. It should be equally obvious, however, that they provide a basis for understanding the conflicting views of judicial authority that have existed throughout the history of our Constitution. By better understanding the sources of that conflict, we may be better able to resolve it in particular circumstances.

The executive clearly has its roots in Machiavelli's prince and Hobbes's sovereign. These roots do much to explain why the executive is the focal point of modern government. But the executive is not the same as either Machiavelli's prince or Hobbes's sovereign—the executive does not possess absolute authority (of course we have seen that the prince and sovereign do not either). The executive's power is circumscribed by law and by the existence of the legislature and the judiciary. But within that sphere the executive still possesses the discretionary authority to act. Moreover, he is the only part of the government that can act. He enforces the laws of the legislature and the decisions of the courts. He is not a mere tool. As Locke states, he can do what is necessary to promote the public interest. Finally, he will be the primary representative of the nation as a whole. But none of these claims should appear to be radical. Would we not want the executive to be able legitimately to do what is necessary to preserve the peace and security of the community? Is the executive not the most logical representative of the unity of the nation?

The essential powers of the executive remain the same as Machiavelli's prince or Hobbes's sovereign, but they are more clearly circumscribed by the consent of the people and the laws. As we have seen, this provides safeguards to the people, but it may also allow for the secure establishment of an executive capable of providing the animating force for modern liberal government.

CHAPTER SEVEN

The Democratic Executive and the Maintenance of Limited Government

Locke and Montesquieu did not provide the last word on the liberal executive. In some important respects their work still exhibited remnants of the premodern monarchy. It was the American Founders who took the final step in the creation of a modern liberal executive. It was they who created the democratic modern Presidency.[1] Both liberal and conservative scholars have erred in the extent to which they have ignored this fact and traced the origins of the democratic Presidency to the Progressive movement.

The Progressive movement did mark the beginning of a transformation in American politics, but the Progressives were not responsible for the democratization of the Presidency. The Progressive transformation of American politics was marked by a depreciation of the Constitution. This took two forms: first, the Progressives ignored the institutional sources of executive strength and restraint provided by the Constitution; second,

---

1. Harvey Mansfield Jr. notes the importance of the popular election of the President in the development of the idea of the executive. See Harvey C. Mansfield Jr., *Taming the Prince: The Ambivalence of Modern Executive Power* (New York: The Free Press, 1989), chap. 10. But Mansfield's analysis of the American executive focuses more on the institutional elements of the American executive than on the popular elements. He explains the importance of the Constitution in providing an institutional basis for executive energy and strength, but he places less emphasis on the strength and legitimacy that result from the innovation of popular election. His analysis draws extensively on the *Federalist* and clearly develops the institutional argument found there. But it says relatively little about the more democratic arguments made by Wilson and Morris at the Constitutional Convention.

they rejected the idea of limited government in favor of the idea of national community. To the extent that the Presidency has changed, we shall see that it is these factors that are responsible for the change.

THE DEMOCRATIC EXECUTIVE AND MODERN POLITICAL THEORY

For Locke and for Montesquieu the executive power was still associated with monarchy. Neither suggests the abolition of monarchy, and neither supports the democratic election of the executive. One might argue that they were creatures of their times, and in one sense that is true. Locke and Montesquieu were political thinkers, but they were not utopians. They sought to improve the existing political arrangements. They accepted democracy, because they believed that the supports for older forms of political authority were fast disappearing. But they may have tolerated monarchy because they did not believe that the tide of democracy would be likely to sweep away the monarchs of their day.

Nor is it obvious that they would have wanted that to happen. Both Locke and Montesquieu understood the difficulty in maintaining a stable democracy capable of self-defense and self-government. They hoped that in the proper constitutional context monarchy could provide the energy and stability that democracies tend to lack. Montesquieu's praise of England may have reflected his practical appreciation of the difficulty of creating a stable democracy, rather than an unalloyed belief in the perfection of its political institutions. England exhibited many of the healthy elements of constitutional government that Montesquieu wanted to promote. It was the best model available for Montesquieu, but it did not necessarily represent the culmination of modern liberal government.

The problem with the English system is that its monarchy is ultimately grounded on a premodern political tradition. Perhaps Locke and Montesquieu hoped that the monarchy supported by tradition would ultimately give way to a monarchy supported by an appreciation of sound administration.[2] Perhaps they believed that if the monarchy could be surrounded by democratic institutions and laws it would be sufficiently restrained so that it would pose no threat to liberal government, and inspire no envy in the people. But if they did, they were in error.

2. In *Federalist* No. 68 Hamilton makes a similar argument, claiming that the Constitution should ultimately be judged on its "aptitude and tendency to produce a good administration." See Alexander Hamilton et al., *The Federalist,* ed. Jacob E. Cooke (Cleveland: Meridian Books, 1961), 461.

The parliamentary systems that continue to dominate England and Europe are the result of a failure to address this problem directly. Monarchy could not continue to exercise real authority without the legitimacy of popular support or election. In some countries the monarch remained to provide a kind of symbolic leadership.[3] In others the monarchy disappeared completely, its functions assumed by an institution that was not designed to perform them.

Parliamentary government represents a case of arrested development in the context of modern liberal government, because parliamentary systems never developed an independent executive power. In parliamentary systems the shadow of traditional monarchy has covered the ground in which an independent and democratic executive might have taken root. It is particularly ironic that so many political scientists have looked to parliamentary systems as a source of progressive reform, when in fact it is the parliamentary system that is regressive.[4] While reformers hold up parliamentary systems as models for unified action, we find that in reality it is parliamentary systems that often exhibit the greatest tendency toward fragmentation.[5] The reason for this is that the parliamentary system is a reactionary response to the problem of monarchy, not a progressive response to the problem of democracy.

If modern liberal government was only a reaction against monarchy, the appeal of parliamentary systems would be more defensible. If we looked only at the most superficial level of the writings of Machiavelli, Hobbes, Locke, and Montesquieu, the case for parliamentary government might seem persuasive. But the problem of modern liberal government is not merely how to kill the king. By the time the early modern thinkers were writing, the traditional monarchy was already dead, or at least in principle

3. The current difficulties of the British monarchy demonstrate the inherent problems with the idea of monarch as figurehead. History and tradition can provide some weight to the monarchy, but eventually the absence of real authority or power will empty the symbolic monarchy of its meaning and purpose.

4. The tendency to look toward parliamentary systems as a progressive alternative to the American constitutional separation of powers has a long and ongoing history. See, for example, Woodrow Wilson, *Congressional Government* (Boston: Houghton Mifflin, 1885); James MacGregor Burns, *The Deadlock of Democracy* (Englewood Cliffs, N.J.: Prentice Hall, 1963); Lloyd N. Cutler, "To Form a Government," *Foreign Affairs* 59 (Fall 1980); and James L. Sundquist, *Constitutional Reform and Effective Government* (Washington, D.C.: The Brookings Institution, 1986). Although none of these thinkers believes it is practical to propose the adoption of a parliamentary system in the United States, they all look to the parliamentary system as the standard for a successful democracy.

5. There are numerous examples of the problems of fragmentation in parliamentary systems. France provides perhaps the best case study. France was able to achieve a stable democracy only when it abandoned its simple parliamentary system for a hybrid system that included a very powerful President.

dying. The real problem for them was how to create an effective government on a democratic foundation. Parliaments served as an effective means of checking monarchical power in the period of transition from monarchy to democracy, but they were never designed to address the more fundamental problem of creating an effective democratic government in the absence of monarchy.

The separation-of-powers doctrine developed by the early modern political thinkers was an attempt to respond to that problem. By explaining that even a democratic government must make room for the energy and unity that traditionally had been supplied by monarchy, these thinkers laid the foundations for the democratic executive. But as Harvey Mansfield Jr. has explained, there was an ambivalence in this early modern idea of executive power. As his title *Taming the Prince* suggests, the prince was to be tamed in order that he might serve in the house of democratic government. But he must also remain free and sometimes even ferocious if democratic government is to succeed. This ambivalence is at the core of the modern executive.[6]

In the systems created by the early modern thinkers, a gulf remained between the people, and the executive who represented the necessity of government power and unity. In Machiavelli and Hobbes the gulf was obvious. In Locke and Montesquieu every attempt was made to camouflage that gulf, but as we have seen in our discussion of Lockean prerogative and Montesquieu's version of the separation of powers, the gulf remained unbridged. It was the American invention of the democratic executive that took the decisive step in uniting executive power and popular government. By creating a popularly elected executive, and thereby giving the executive its own source of legitimacy in popular opinion, the executive power is reconciled with democratic principles.

The solution seems so simple in retrospect that we wonder why it was not proposed sooner. Perhaps an odd combination of the fears of monarchy and the fears of democracy was responsible for the delay. Opponents of monarchy feared the energy and strength popular election would convey on the executive, whereas those distrustful of democracy feared the potential for demagoguery and shortsightedness in a system dominated by a simple national election. Another contribution of the American Founders to the doctrine of liberal government—the written constitution—takes account of both of those fears.

The written U.S. Constitution creates competing institutional mechanisms for the expression of popular will. The popular voice will be filtered

6. Mansfield, *Taming the Prince*, xv–xxiv.

through the legislature as well as the executive, because it is first filtered through the Constitution. The President will have a claim to popular legitimacy, but not the only claim. In addition, the President's exercise of power will be checked by the restraints of the laws passed by the legislature as well as by the restraints of the written constitution itself.

The constitutional structure will not only serve to check and restrain executive power, but also provide institutional sources of authority that will allow the President to resist public opinion and the legislature. In the absence of a written constitution, the legitimacy of the President's actions would rest either on immediate popular support or on the expression of the popular will as embodied in the laws passed by the legislature. The written constitution provides an alternative. Under a written constitution the President's ultimate claim to legal authority comes not from the legislature but from the constitution itself. The President's claim to legal authority is equal to that of the legislature's because it comes from the same source.

In spite of their best efforts, the early modern political theorists were unable to reconcile the need for executive strength and independence with the ideas of limited government and the rule of law. Even Locke's complex defense of both legislative supremacy and the prerogative power was ultimately unsatisfactory. Locke reduced the tension between Hobbes's "absolute" sovereign and the idea of limited government, but he did not succeed in creating a lasting harmony between them. Limited government cannot defend itself without prerogative power, but prerogative power threatens the existence of limited government. Limited government and prerogative power are trapped in a perverse relationship where each element needs the other, but when they are brought together they conflict.

Under the American Constitution executive power and the rule of law are reconciled. Just as the doctrines of legislative supremacy and prerogative power arise together, so to do the existence of a popular independent executive and a written constitution. The American President is subservient to the law of the Constitution. He is checked by the political forces created by the constitutional separation of powers. But he also has discretionary authority and a claim to popular legitimacy established by the Constitution. The Presidency actually gains strength from the Constitution, and the Constitution is more secure because of the existence of the Presidency.

The American Constitution and the American Presidency are the culmination of the efforts of the early modern political theorists. It is through these institutional innovations that the ideas of limited government and executive power at last join hands. The political realism of the early modern philosophers finds its ultimate expression in the practical creation of the American political system.

THE AMERICAN PROBLEM WITH THE AMERICAN SYSTEM

The failure to appreciate this American invention is exhibited not only in the ideas of European and American defenders of parliamentary government, but also in the more indigenous versions of the doctrine of legislative supremacy. The popular ideal of legislative supremacy finds its American origins in the civics book vision of the New England town meeting. The New England town meeting is the archetype of democracy in action. There citizens come together to make the decisions that will govern their political community. They literally govern themselves through the town meeting.

Few people believe that such a system is possible in a nation the size of the United States, but it remains the standard by which alternative systems are judged. It is this standard that is at the core of the whig view of government. The people cannot come together to legislate for themselves, but they can send representatives to legislate in their name. The legislature is supreme because it is the proxy for actual self-government. Other branches of government may exist, but they must be subservient to the legislature because it is the legislature that represents the sovereign will of the people.

This whig view of American government has found expression throughout our history, although that expression has typically been in reaction to the governing initiatives of others. The anti-Federalist critics of the Constitution often appealed to the fear of executive tyranny in any government that departed from the principle of legislative supremacy. The Jeffersonians wanted to wrest power from what they saw as an increasingly "imperial" executive. Appropriately, the most systematic defense of the doctrine of legislative supremacy was developed by members of the Whig party, including Henry Clay and Daniel Webster, in response to the executive initiatives of Andrew Jackson. And much of the Whigs' argument for legislative supremacy was resurrected by critics of Lincoln, Andrew Johnson, Theodore Roosevelt, Wilson, and Franklin Roosevelt.

Despite the pervasiveness of this ideal of government in the American mind, we have seen that American history presents another side of the picture. Americans have accepted, even welcomed, the exercise of broad discretionary powers on the part of the executive. From Lincoln's suspension of the writ of habeas corpus during the Civil War, to the exclusion of the Japanese from the West Coast during World War II, the President has been allowed the widest latitude to act in what he believed to be the national interest in times of emergency. Even such a staunch defender of the whig doctrine of legislative supremacy as Thomas Jefferson negotiated the purchase of the Louisiana Territory without prior congressional approval because he believed such a purchase to be in the national interest.

The exercise of these so-called prerogative powers is certainly the most dramatic and most often cited example of the failure of the political system to live up to the ideal of legislative supremacy, but it may not be the most important example. As we have seen, there is a natural if uneasy kinship between the doctrine of legislative supremacy and the exercise of prerogative powers. The bigger threat to the doctrine of legislative supremacy may come not from extraordinary executive actions but from the rise of the administrative state. Many of the authoritative decisions made by government today are made not by the legislature but by the bureaucracy. No one denies the existence of the administrative state, and no one seriously thinks that it can be eliminated. But it is also quite clear that the existence of the administrative state is at odds with the doctrine of legislative supremacy.

Finally, whig political theory and American political practice are at odds with regard to domestic-policy initiation. According to this theory, the branch of government that makes the laws should be the primary source of domestic policy. The legislature can in no way be regarded as supreme if the policy agenda is controlled by another branch. But again, if we look to the practice of American politics we find that major shifts in public policy are almost always identified with particular Presidents, not with particular Congresses. Congress plays a major role in domestic-policy formation, but it rarely plays the role of agenda setter. It is the President who is the foremost popular leader and the foremost legislative leader in our political system. Our practice cannot be explained by the whig theory of government.

PROGRESSIVISM AND THE CONSTITUTION

The contemporary idea of the modern Presidency arose in response to the gap between the theory and practice of American politics. The whig interpretation of the Constitution supported by constitutional scholars such as Corwin created a void that could be filled only by recourse to an extraconstitutional theory of political development—the theory of the modern Presidency.[7] But that theory in turn relies heavily on the theory of democracy developed by the Progressives at the turn of the century.

We have already seen that Progressive thinkers and statesmen incorporated all the elements of the modern Presidency into their political thought and political action, but we have also seen that they were not unique or original in this respect. We have traced the elements identified with the modern Presidency back through the Presidencies of Lincoln, Jackson, and Washington, to the Constitution itself. It is not the Constitution that is inconsistent with the President's popular leadership, legislative initiative, administrative discretion, and independent executive action; it is only the whig theory of the Constitution that is inconsistent with such practice. The Progressives did not transform the office of the Presidency in its relation to Congress, but they did transform our understanding of the constitutional framework within which the office operated, and in so doing provided the theoretical underpinnings for the contemporary myth of the modern Presidency.

First of all, like the contemporary proponents of the theory of the modern Presidency, the Progressives believed that a powerful modern Presidency could exist only if the President escaped the constraints of the Constitution. They accepted the whig theory of the Constitution that was popular in the nineteenth century, and they concluded that any Constitution based on such a narrow conception of executive power would be inadequate for the needs of the twentieth century. Popular legitimacy, administrative support, and extralegal authority were the keys to a strong Presidency for the Progressives, and they assumed, following the whigs, that these elements could not be found within the Constitution.

The Progressives ignored the desirability and need for institutional sources of strength and authority, and they failed to see the potential instability of simple direct democracy as the sole support for presidential authority. The Progressives "recovered" the democratic elements of the Presidency only by wrenching them from their constitutional origins and denying them the complementary support of institutional authority. The Progressive idea led us to believe that elements of the modern Presidency could only exist outside the Constitution.[8]

Second, the Progressives attempted to transform the idea of the ends of democratic government. It was not just the constraints of the separation

7. Edward S. Corwin, *The President: Office and Powers* (New York: New York University Press, 1940).

8. It is understandable that the strong constitutional Presidency school discussed in Chapter 2 (Storing, Ceaser, Tulis, et al.) deemphasized the democratic sources of strength in the constitutional Presidency. They wanted to show there were institutional sources of authority that the reigning Progressive orthodoxy failed to appreciate.

of powers that the Progressives thought must be escaped; it was the very notion of limited constitutional government. The Constitution, they thought, placed limits on the will of democracy and prevented the government from responding to the needs of the people. At its most fundamental level the Progressives wanted to transform the American political system from one that protects individual rights to one that promotes the growth of national community. Once the idea of rights had been replaced by the idea of community, once the limits of constitutional government were replaced by the legitimacy of unchecked popular leadership, the "promise of American life" could be fulfilled.[9]

Although the Progressives might have found the power to deal with their immediate political problems within the Constitution, they once again accepted their opponents' constitutional theories. They assumed that limited constitutional government should be equated with a radical version of the laissez-faire doctrine. Thus they turned to the idea of national community to justify a more active role for the national government. With or without the Progressives' theory of national community, the twentieth century would inevitably have seen tremendous growth in activity on the part of the national government in general and the President in particular. But what the Progressives did was suggest the possibility of an unlimited expansion of government power. Once the legitimate scope of government activity breaks the bounds of constitutional limits, there is little to check the growth of government. Democracy is at last free from the "bondage of law."[10]

The Imperial Presidency and the Progressive Presidency

Those who complain about the growth of presidential power fail to distinguish between a powerful constitutional Presidency and a powerful Progressive Presidency. They are typically guilty of two errors. First, they fail to see that the power of the modern Presidency is not the power of a king.[11] The principle of democracy, not the principle of monarchy, has been used to legitimate the growth of Presidential power. Although we

9. For the best statement of the Progressive thought, see Herbert Croly, *The Promise of American Life* (Cambridge, Mass.: Harvard University Press, 1965).

10. Croly describes the goal of the Progressives as the emancipation "of democracy from the bondage of law." See Herbert Croly, *Progressive Democracy* (New York: Macmillan Co., 1915), 14.

11. This criticism is directed at the contemporary critics of the "imperial Presidency." See esp. Arthur M. Schlesinger Jr., *The Imperial Presidency* (New York: Popular Library, 1973).

have seen that the Founders themselves wanted to provide a democratic source of legitimacy for the Presidency, they also saw the need to provide constitutional limits on the exercise of all forms of political power. By separating the democratic Presidency from the constitutional Presidency, the Progressives eliminated the basis for restraint. The Progressive Presidency needs no limits, because for the Progressives democracy needs no limits. Thus it is partisans of democracy, not the partisans of a strong constitutional Presidency, who seek unlimited presidential power.

Second, many of the criticisms of the growth of executive power have been misplaced. Does the President wield too much discretionary authority? Does he control too large an administrative staff? Does he actively promote too broad a legislative agenda? One might answer yes to all of these questions but not find the source of that problem in the growth of executive power vis-à-vis the other branches of government. The problem is instead the growth of government as a whole. In a government whose activities are as wide-ranging as ours, there is no substitute for the modern Presidency as it exists. The President provides the unity and energy that allows such a system to function. This was true with the more limited government of the nineteenth century, and it remains true today. If the system does not function as well today, it is the size of the government as a whole that is responsible, not the size of the Presidency.

To the contrary, the Presidency may offer one of the greatest possible sources of protection for the doctrine of limited government. As we mentioned in the Introduction, there has been a tendency to identify proponents of a more active Presidency with proponents of a more active national government, but there have been important exceptions. In addition to Andrew Jackson, Ronald Reagan certainly comes to mind as an example of an activist President who supported the idea and practice of limited government. Both believed in using the powers of their office to restrain what they saw as the unchecked growth of the national government, and to reestablish an appreciation for the constitutional concept of limited government.

But if expanding the national government is a sure way of expanding the power of the Presidency, why would any President resist such an expansion? Perhaps because when faced with the need to exercise the powers of the Presidency it becomes obvious that less is sometimes more. What Greenstein learned from Eisenhower he might have learned from Machiavelli, or any of the other early modern theorists.[12] The doctrine of limited government teaches that government should not do more than is necessary to maintain the peace and security of the community. This may

---

12. Fred I. Greenstein, *The Hidden-Hand Presidency* (New York: Basic Books, 1982).

still be quite a lot, but by limiting the tasks of government the task of governing becomes more manageable. What Greenstein might also have learned from these early modern thinkers is that the solution cannot be a mere lowering of expectations for the Presidency, but it must be a lowering of expectations for the government as a whole. A more modest Presidency in the face of a more immodest government would be a recipe for disaster, for it is primarily through the Presidency that the activity of the government gains coherence and direction.

Even a limited government requires a powerful executive if it is to function effectively. Contrary to what many contemporary conservatives believe, limited government is not a synonym for weak government. What the authors of the Constitution and the early modern political theorists recognized is that a limited government must be a powerful government, and it can be that only if there is adequate provision for the exercise of executive power.

The Progressives may have been partially justified in their search outside the Constitution for a source of authority and direction. Because conservatives of their day often confused the idea of limited government with a kind of libertarianism, the Progressives naturally looked outside the framework of the Constitution in order to address the problems that they faced. They looked outside the Constitution for a source of governmental authority and executive power. They relinquished the ground of constitutional legitimacy to the proponents of a libertarian whig political theory. The libertarian whig perspective remains a part of the American political tradition, but it is a part that refuses to recognize the exigencies of government. Its advocates are trapped in an adolescent reaction against government authority and executive power, unable to proceed to a mature reflection on the problems of democratic government. But in their reaction against the reactionaries, the Progressives also lost sight of the full dimensions of the problem. The libertarian whigs cannot escape the belief that government should do as little as possible, while the Progressives are blinded by the belief that government can do virtually everything.

The American Constitution offers an alternative to both perspectives. It shows that the doctrine of limited government is truly a middle ground between tyranny and anarchy. At the center of that Constitution is the office of the Presidency. The discretionary powers of the office remind us that self-government is ultimately impossible. We can never escape the need for some people to exercise discretionary authority over others. The democratic base of the Presidency reminds us that, in the proper institutional setting, democratic government need not degenerate into either the rule of the mob or the rule of the tyrant.

Index